GLEN BRETON RARE (38)
GLENFARCLAS 105 (40)
GLENFIDDICH 30y.o (42)
GLENGLASSAUGH (43)
GLEN GLASSAUGH 26y.o (44
GREENSPOT (48)
Thomas H HANDY (50)
HIBIKI 30y.o (53)
HIGHLAND PARK 40y.o (57)
JOHNNIE WALKER BLUE LABEL
KING GEORGE V EDITION (61)
MACKMYRA (67)
MAKER'S MARK (68)
MELLOW CORN (69)
REDBREAST (75)
SHEEP DIP (77)
SPEYBURN (79)
ST GEORGES (81)
MACALLAN FINEOAK 30y.o (91)
THE TYRCONNEL (94)
TOBERMORY 15y.o (95)
VAN WINKLE FAMILY RESERVE RYE (96)
WILD TURKEY RARE BREED (97)
WOODFORD RESERVE 98

Ian Buxton

101 Whiskies to Try Before You Die

ARDBEG Uigeadail (6)
BASIL HAYDEN's (11)
BENRIACH CURIOSITAS PEATED (12)
BERNHEIM (14)
BLUE HANGER (18)
BNJ (19)
BUFFALO TRACE (22)
CAMERON BRIG (25)
CHIVAS REGAL (27)
CROWN ROYAL (29)
CUTTY SARK 25yo (31)
DEWARS SIGNATURE (33)
EAGLE RARE (36)
~~ELIJAH~~
ELIJAH CRAIG (37)

37

Also by Ian Buxton:

The Enduring Legacy of Dewar's

Glenglassaugh: A Distillery Reborn

Ian Buxton

101 Whiskies to Try Before You Die

First published in 2010
by HACHETTE SCOTLAND, an imprint of HACHETTE UK
1

Cataloguing in Publication Data is available from the British Library

978 0 7553 6083 3

Designed by Republic Productions
www.republicproductions.com

Printed and bound by Butler Tanner and Dennis Ltd

Hachette Scotland's policy is to use papers that are natural, renewable and recyclable products and made from wood grown in sustainable forests. The logging and manufacturing processes are expected to conform to the environmental regulations of the country of origin.

HACHETTE SCOTLAND
An Hachette UK Company
338 Euston Road
London NW1 3BH

www.headline.co.uk
www.hachette.co.uk

Contents

Introduction

101 Whiskies to Try Before You Die is a whisky list with a difference. Accessible whisky for real people.

It is not an awards list.

It is not a list of the 101 'best' whiskies in the world.

It is simply, as it says in the title, a guide to 101 whiskies that enthusiasts really should seek out and try – love them or hate them – to complete their whisky education. What's more, it's practical and realistic.

101 Whiskies to Try Before You Die does not contain obscure single-cask bottlings that sold out weeks before publication and it doesn't contain hugely expensive whiskies that virtually no one can afford to buy anyway (even if they could find them).

After all, what's the point? I might look terrifically smart recommending, say, the Glenglassaugh 40 Years Old that recently won the International Wine & Spirit Competition's special trophy for 40 Years Old Scotch Whisky. By one token at least, that makes it the very best single malt Scotch you can buy. A panel of really well-informed and expert judges (not just one person and not me) picked it from its peers. Though little known, it is very, very good and I could be seen to be doing you a favour by pointing you its way. But it's £1,500 a bottle. Or perhaps, Glenfiddich's 50 Years Old, a snip at £10,000. Are you really going to nip out and buy a bottle? I don't think so. So I set myself some rules when I started writing this book.

Essentially, they can be summed up as: every whisky listed here must be a) generally available (although you might have to look a little bit, every one of these whiskies should be available from a decent whisky specialist or through an online retailer) and b) affordable (read on to see what that means). And, though it goes without saying, there must be a reason for their inclusion. Mostly it's because they're very, very good examples of their kind, but sometimes they deserve your support for other reasons. Sometimes it will be because they are made by small distillers swimming against a tide of corporate ubiquity but it might just be because a particular whisky is simply so unusual that you just have to try it. That might mean reminding you of something familiar that you knew about but had, sort of, forgotten; hopefully, more often, it will point you to something new, unexpected and surprising.

Above all, this book is about whiskies to drink, not collect.

So I've excluded one-off bottlings or single-cask releases, because there's simply not enough to go around. And I've simply ignored whiskies that seem to me to be designed primarily for collectors. Perhaps more importantly, I've taken a very hard-headed look at retail prices. I've been highly selective once a whisky rises above £100 in a typical British whisky shop; very critical indeed if it costs £500 or more, and flatly ignored it once the price breaks the £1,000 barrier. So, sorry The Macallan 57 Year Old Finest Cut in your Lalique crystal decanter; goodbye Dalmore 62 Year Old and farewell to Ardbeg's ritzy Double Barrel. Tasty though you may be, your fantasy price tags rule you out. Let's get real: this book is for whisky drinkers, not Russian plutocrats.

What's more, because I don't believe in the simplistic and reductionist notion of the 'world's best whisky', everything's in alphabetical order.

And even more unusually, nothing has a 'score'. Again, I simply don't accept that you should follow one person's individual preferences and more or less idiosyncratic scoring system (and that's all that most tasting books are). There are several reasons why I believe 100-point scoring systems don't work, not least the idea that any one individual can consistently and reliably differentiate between a whisky scoring 92 and one scoring 93. It seems to me palpably absurd, so we're not going there.

Better, in fact, to take some advice from Aeneas MacDonald, the original sage of whisky, who in 1930 suggested that the discerning drinker learn to judge whisky with 'his mother-wit, his nose and his palate to guide him'. Sound words.

But, so many whiskies so little time. With the world of whisky expanding almost daily, an experienced guide may be of some value, if only to point you in new directions and suggest some unexplored and rewarding byways that you may not have considered. Scotch, American, Irish, Japanese and Canadian whiskies are all in here. As are some from Sweden and other unexpected producing nations.

So I have strenuously attempted to be wide-ranging in my approach and, so far as I am able, to include some whiskies that I personally don't particularly care for but which are regarded as exemplars of their kind.

So how, you may ask, did I assemble this list?

There is no one answer.

First, I used my own knowledge and judgement. I have worked in the whisky industry for more than 20 years; consulted for a number of distillers; been Marketing Director for one of Scotland's leading single malt whiskies; created and run the World Whiskies Conference; written widely about whisky; and sat on a number of competition judging panels. So, though I'm still learning about whisky and there's something new to discover almost daily, I'm privileged to have tried a lot of different whiskies and reckon to know something about them and the people who made them.

Secondly, I looked at what my peers think. Mainly I've looked at the major award winners at important international competitions such as the International Wine & Spirit Competition (IWSC); the San Francisco World Spirits Competition; *Whisky Magazine*'s World Whiskies Awards (from time to time I'm on the judging panel for that one); and more informal awards such as that from the Malt Maniacs. Tasting notes by such luminaries as F. Paul Pacult and those appearing in the various international whisky magazines have all served to draw different whiskies to my attention.

And finally, I asked some of my whisky friends and colleagues to nominate their favourites – in the case of practising distillers they had to nominate at least one of their competitors' whiskies for every one of their own, and the same rules on cost and availability were applied. Those who helped are listed in the acknowledgements page – many thanks to them. But I should explain that I used my whisky friends rather like the ancient Greeks used the Oracles – I've listened to the advice, but the final choices were mine. So blame me if you don't agree with the list.

As I write this there are, entirely coincidentally, 101 whisky distilleries operating in the UK where I live (yes, there are at least two outside Scotland), but such is the constantly changing nature of this industry that the number will be wrong by the time you read this. Around the world there are – oh, I don't know, perhaps two hundred or so. Probably more.

And they keep opening. One of the exciting things about the whisky industry in the last ten years has been the proliferation of new distilleries across the world, especially boutique craft distilleries in 'new' whisky-producing countries. Many have excellent and informative visitor centres – but opening hours and seasons vary. Because of that, I haven't given specific details but suggest you check online or phone in advance to confirm when they are open.

We can now get whisky from Scotland, Ireland, Canada, the USA, Japan, India, Sweden, Belgium, Switzerland, Australia, France, Austria, the Czech Republic, England, Wales, Finland, Germany, Holland, Russia, New Zealand, Pakistan, Turkey, South Korea and South Africa. Apparently, there are even whisky distilleries in Brazil, Nepal, Uruguay and Venezuela. Inevitably, more than half the whiskies in this book are single malts from Scotland, with Scottish blends and grains taking the total from my home country to an impressive 72 whiskies. But, reflecting the growing popularity, influence and quality of 'world whiskies', more than a quarter of those I have selected are from the USA, Japan and other countries – and I can assure you that you'll be impressed.

So, when you consider that all of these countries can produce any number of 'single malt' expressions differentiated by age, cask type, finish and so forth, and most of them do, and then add blended whiskies and indigenous non-Scotch styles, such as bourbon, rye and so on, to the potential universe, you can see that tasting them represents a lifetime of unremitting toil.

One of the lessons of this book is that you don't have to spend a lot of money to find really great or interesting whiskies. In fact, I didn't really look at price until after completing the first draft of the list. The price ranges indicated in the text are based on the typical UK retail price from a specialist independent whisky shop, and were correct as we went to press. Around half are under £40. In fact, if you bought a bottle of everything here it would cost around £7,100, if you were in the UK (but you'd probably be able to negotiate a discount). If you dropped the three most expensive the rest would average just over £56 a bottle – go compare that with the world's best-known wines. Whisky can be a serious bargain!

Here's the key to the 1 to 5 scale:
1 Under £25 2 £25–40 3 £40–69 4 £70–150 5 Over £150

Of course, prices change all the time. In particular, tax and duty rates change, products are put on promotion or, generally less favourably for the consumer, 'repositioned' as the marketing folks would have it. Prices will also vary if you are reading this thousands of miles away from me in a place where costs may be higher for long-distance imports, but less for local bottles.

High rates of taxation in the UK come as a constant surprise to visitors from many countries, however, who regularly ask 'why is whisky more expensive here in Scotland than in my home?' For the answer, apply to the Government who, at the time of writing, take around three-quarters of the retail price of a bottle of standard Scotch whisky in excise duty and VAT.

There are several thousand whiskies out there – perhaps even ten thousand. No one really knows. So, as the old joke would have it, it's tough work but someone has to do it. I've picked 101 for you to enjoy, saving you hours of joyless labour. You don't have to thank me; buying the book will do just fine.

Each one has an entry describing the whisky and the producer, with some background information that I hope you'll find useful and interesting. Then there are brief tasting notes. These are not intended to be the be-all-and-end-all, more a jumping-off point for your own exploration and to help explain why each whisky made the cut. You'll also find a space to record your own purchases, personal favourites and tasting notes.

Within these pages I hope you'll find a few surprises, perhaps a few old favourites and also some bargains. I hope you'll be inspired to try something new and share what you learn with a few friends. This isn't by any stretch of imagination the completely definitive whisky list. Despite what others may say, I doubt that such a thing can exist. But it will take you on a wonderful journey of discovery and exploration and, if you manage to try all 101 whiskies, then you can die happy.

I'd be interested to hear what you think of the list and what whiskies you'd suggest for inclusion in a future edition. Email me at feedback@101whiskies.com

Meanwhile, sláinte!

1

Producer	John Dewar & Sons Ltd
Distillery	Aberfeldy, Perthshire
Visitor Centre	Yes
Availability	Widespread international availability
Price	□□□■□

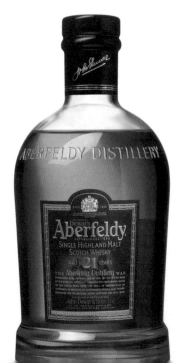

www.dewars.com

Aberfeldy
21 Years Old

It's a great shame this isn't more widely known because I'm willing to guess that people who 'don't like whisky' would like this and people who know and like whisky would like it a lot.

The Dewar's distillery at Aberfeldy was built from 1896–98 by the restless, innovative and entrepreneurial Dewar brothers, Tommy and John, who hired Charles Cree Doig, the finest distillery architect who ever lived, to design it for them. But, for years, under the ownership of the old Distillers Company Ltd, all of the output went for blending and the single malt boom passed Aberfeldy by.

However, in one of the periodic convulsive reorganisations that the Scotch whisky industry indulges in to keep bankers and lawyers in expensive German motor cars, in March 1998 ownership was transferred to Bacardi who, up until then, had only had a minor interest in whisky. The result was a wave of investment, including what has been described by *Whisky Magazine* as 'the ultimate Scotch whisky visitor centre' and a number of exciting new products.

The best of these is this 21 Years Old single malt. Aberfeldy is noted for a gentle, heather-honey sweetness and this whisky is just delightful: well-mannered, delicate and surprisingly complex. It's a shame about the rather squat and ugly bottle but don't let that put you off.

It may be easier to find the 12 Year Old version – that's good, but this is a lot better and well worth the additional money. The extra age really rounds out and deepens this whisky, the subtlety of which would tragically get lost in a blending vat.

Colour Warm gold and amber.
Nose A creamy, honeyed nose with dried fruits, heather flowers and hints of coconut.
Taste Intense but not cloying sweetness, dark orange marmalade, vanilla and oak wood. Mouth coating and creamy.
Finish This is long, quite spicy and has hints of lemon. Restrained and elegant.

Verdict

2

Producer	Chivas Brothers Ltd
Distillery	Aberlour, Speyside
Visitor Centre	Yes
Availability	Specialists, better supermarkets and duty free
Price	☐■☐☐☐

✓

www.aberlour.com

Aberlour

a'bunadh

A cask strength whisky has quietly been making a name for itself over the past few years and has now attracted quite a crowd of enthusiastic devotees who praise the big, rich flavours of this Speyside malt.

Aberlour distillery was established in 1879 and then remodelled by the leading distillery architect Charles Doig some twenty years later after a disastrous fire. It really came into its own after 1975 when it was acquired by the French group Pernod Ricard and became their lead single malt brand in the days before their purchase of the Seagram distilleries (The Glenlivet in particular). Today the distillery offers an excellent 'Aberlour Distillery Experience' tour which is well worth making the effort to take (booking is essential).

There are several easily accessible expressions, and the possibility of bottling your own direct from a single cask at the distillery, but the one to go for is the strangely named a'bunadh (it's pronounced a-boon-ah and means 'the origin' in Gaelic). It is non-chill filtered and at full-cask strength, the idea behind the product being to replicate a 19th-century-style whisky matured exclusively in Spanish oak oloroso sherry butts. So, if you like traditional Macallan or Glenfarclas, you're going to love this.

Note that this is released in batches, some of which have been criticised as tasting slightly sulphured (an effect of cask treatment), so if you find a batch that you particularly like, it might be an idea to snap up several bottles before it runs out. Equally, it's fun to keep experimenting and, perhaps, taste one batch against another. And this shouldn't be a problem, because, for whisky of this quality and strength (it's usually around the 60% abv mark), it's quite a bargain. Expect to pay about £35.

Colour Rich and dark.

Nose A marked sherry character, possibly honey and dark fruits.

Taste Can be drunk at full strength but develops with water. Big, mouth filling, Christmas cake, dried fruits, possibly some citrus and chocolate notes.

Finish Expect a drawn-out finish, perhaps with evolving spices, oak and some smoky notes.

Verdict

3

Producer
Distillery
Visitor Centre
Availability
Price

Amrut Distilleries Ltd
Amrut, Bangalore, India
No
Specialists

www.amrutwhisky.com

Amrut
Fusion

Indian whisky? Some mistake, surely? Well, no. India is a huge whisky market and a giant producer but, unfortunately, the vast majority of Indian whisky is made from molasses – and so far as the EU is concerned that means it's rum and can't be sold as 'whisky'.

This is currently the basis of a major and long-running trade dispute, with the Scotch whisky industry claiming that Indian import duties are an illegal restraint of trade, and the Indian producers crying foul and pointing out that much of their distilling industry was set up by the British in the first place. Today, the Indian industry is dominated by Vijay Mallya's United Spirits, producers of such fine brands as Bagpiper and McDowells. To add to the confusion, they also own Glasgow's Whyte & Mackay. But the Indian whisky that has made it into this list is actually distilled by their smaller independent rival, Amrut Distilleries Ltd, established in 1948. According to Indian mythology, when the Gods and the Rakshasas (demons) churned the oceans using the mountain Meru, a golden pot called the 'Amrut' sprang out containing the Elixir of Life.

Amrut is real single malt whisky; that is to say, it is made simply with malted barley, water and yeast so it can be sold here. And that's our good fortune, because it's really very good (you didn't think it was here just out of curiosity, did you?).

Fusion is an unusual product, unique in that it combines Indian barley from the Himalayas with peated malt from Scotland and is bottled at a healthy 50% abv. And despite that (and despite having come halfway round the world), it's pretty good value at a typical £35 a bottle. Just try not to think of the carbon footprint if you're drinking it in Tannochbrae!

Colour Bright gold. Indian whisky matures faster than Scotch so spends less time in the cask.

Nose A pronounced wood impact, but also peat, vanilla and fruit.

Taste Surprisingly complex and engaging, the peat mixes with oak, fruit, chocolate and caramel shortcake.

Finish Yes, you will finish this and want to find another bottle. Fades to a dry spiciness.

Verdict

4

Producer	Inver House Distillers Ltd
Distillery	Knockdhu, Knock, nr Keith, Speyside
Visitor Centre	None – visits by appointment
Availability	Specialists and online
Price	▢■■▢▢

www.ancnoc.com

anCnoc
16 Years Old

You really have to think that Inver House have made life unnecessarily hard for themselves by rebranding Knockdhu as the strange and unpronounceable anCnoc, a Gaelic word meaning 'the hill'. This bestowed upon the whisky the unenviable distinction of no longer being named after the distillery that produces it, but it was apparently done to avoid confusion with Knockando.

It seems a shame, because there is much to commend the Speyside single malts from this little-known distillery between Keith and Banff; in particular, its resolutely traditional style of operation (something of a signature with Inver House). An old-fashioned, cast-iron mash tun is still used, while wooden washbacks made from Douglas fir are favoured over modern stainless steel. More importantly, tradition is also proudly maintained by the continued use of a worm tub, one of just thirteen still in operation across all of Scotland, helping to give anCnoc its depth, body and characteristic rich, meaty aroma.

A mild curiosity about the distillery is that it housed troops from the Indian army during World War 2, along with their mules and horses. Apparently, the local residents would turn out to watch cavalry practice – what the riders thought of this is not recorded!

The 16 Years Old is a relatively recent release, and a welcome one. Unusually it is exclusively matured in ex-bourbon casks, resulting in its deceptively pale colour. The age is apparent on both the nose and palate, however, and this is a complex and satisfying whisky, more robust than the appearance would lead you to expect. Inver House are to be commended for releasing this at 46% abv and not chill filtering the whisky. Hopefully it will achieve wider distribution and greater fame.

Colour Quite pale and straw-like.
Nose Slightly medicinal; lemon zest; vanilla takes over.
Taste Vanilla, liquorice and spice notes; toffee and marmalade.
Finish Drifts gently to a dry conclusion. Holds together well.

Verdict

5

Producer	Glenmorangie plc
Distillery	Ardbeg, Islay
Visitor Centre	Yes
Availability	Widespread international availability
Price	☐■☐☐☐

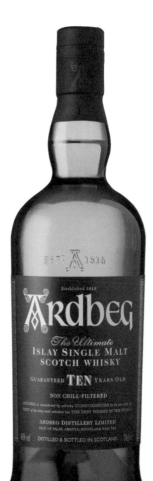

www.ardbeg.com

Ardbeg
10 Years Old

I can't really make my mind up about Ardbeg. I love the place, admire what's been done there and acknowledge the legions of passionate fans who have supported this iconic Islay distillery since it reopened in 1997. It also has the best food of any distillery visitor centre I can call to mind.

But I also feel it's overly pleased with itself. Personally, I find the faux 'homespun' tone of much of their promotion grates with me, especially as it seems to me that it implies that this is some tiny independent struggling for survival against ruthless corporate giants, when in fact it's owned by one of the biggest luxury goods companies on the planet (Louis Vuitton Moet Hennessy). And don't get me started on the ludicrous 'luxury' nonsense which is Ardbeg's £10,000 Double Barrel. It's simply absurd.

However, there's no denying that the current team have done an excellent job and Ardbeg does produce some deeply loved whiskies, as long as you like them peaty. For, this is arguably the benchmark Islay whisky, against which all others must be judged and, for that, we'll forgive it a lot.

The standard is the 'entry-level' Ten Years Old expression which critics have raved about. The stills at Ardbeg differ from others on Islay, being taller and having a curious purifier on the spirit still, the combination of which contributes to the finesse and delicacy of what is a very highly peated spirit. Certainly this is truly complex whisky and, love it or hate it, you just have to explore its finer, non-chilled nuances at least once.

Colour A pale, straw-coloured whisky, set off by the elegant, tall, green glass bottle.

Nose Monstrously peaty, of course, but with attractive citrus notes; cinnamon and pears.

Taste The initial attack of the peat slowly gives way to cereal and barley notes; tobacco, coffee, liquorice and chocolate.

Finish Smoky and slightly sweet; hints of barley linger and you may find some vanilla notes.

Verdict

Producer	Glenmorangie plc
Distillery	Ardbeg, Islay
Visitor Centre	Yes
Availability	International specialist outlets
Price	■■■□□

www.ardbeg.com

Ardbeg
Uigeadail

Having expressed my personal reservations about Ardbeg in the previous entry, I really should, in all fairness, add that at least one highly regarded commentator considers this one of the very best whiskies in the world and, year after year, pours almost unlimited praise on it.

Well, fair enough if you like strong, peaty whiskies. The impossible-to-pronounce Uigeadail (it's named after the loch from which the distillery draws water) is both peaty and very strong (54.2% abv). Certainly, it's been a massive success and has gone down very well with Ardbeg's growing international fan club, so let's acknowledge its appeal.

However, be warned – this is a monster. Full of peat smoke, earthiness and layers of oak, oil, more peat (constantly evolving), it is liable to dominate anything else you drink that day. So save this for the last dram or two of the evening and savour a truly mighty whisky. It is definitely one to explore.

But, being old enough to remember when this style of whisky could hardly be given away, I do have a wider concern. Ardbeg and Port Ellen weren't closed, and other Islay distilleries put on reduced working, on a whim – blenders found that a little goes a long way and those single malt drinkers that were around at the time felt much the same. There is an element of fashion in the current wave of enthusiasm for very highly peated whiskies and, if the enthusiasts who are buying this were ever to move on, then there could be embarrassing quantities of next-to-unsaleable whisky lying in Scotland's warehouses.

You probably don't agree. Just think about it, is all I ask. Meanwhile, enjoy this and savour all its glorious extremity.

Colour Quite pale and straw coloured.
Nose Hints of fino sherry, peat and slightly damp leather.
Taste Multi-layered and intense, creamy/oily, peat smoke and lingering fires; earthy yet sweet. Dried fruits.
Finish Very dominant; intriguing, layered finish with spice hints; sweetness but ultimately drying.

Verdict

7

Producer	Compass Box Whisky Company
Distillery	n/a – this is a blending house
Visitor Centre	n/a
Availability	Mainly UK, USA and France – but check online
Price	☐■☐☐☐

ASYLA

MALT & GRAIN
BLENDED SCOTCH WHISKY

Finesse, Softness & Sweetness
on the palate. Our multiple award-winning 'Asyla'
is made from perfectly mature malt and grain
whiskies from hand-picked American oak casks.
· John Glaser, Whiskymaker.

COMPASS BOX
WHISKY COMPANY

40%vol PRODUCT OF SCOTLAND 70cl

www.compassboxwhisky.com

Asyla

I'd really like to recommend all of the Compass Box whiskies, but that would be cheating, so I've picked three typical of their style and approach. Asyla is the first. If that seems to favour disproportionately what is still a boutique operation, even as it enters its second decade, you need to understand that this is a rather different whisky company – a specialist blending house rather than a distiller – driven by the messianic John Glaser, an anglophile American who started his whisky career with Diageo but opened his own 'house' in 2000, literally blending his first offerings in his own home.

It is possible to tire of the consciously funky names. Personally speaking, I find the style of Compass Box's website overly self-congratulatory and the insistence on their renegade style and fearless outsider stance can sometimes grate (Glaser's business card once carried the title 'Whisky Zealot'; as his countrymen would say, 'Oh, puh-lease . . .'). But that misses the point.

As a stack of awards will testify, Compass Box is revered by whisky's chattering classes and is precious close to becoming part of the whisky establishment (they might deny this) and they've got there by making very, very good whisky indeed. But they don't, in fact, make anything – what they do is blend superb small batch whiskies from very, very carefully selected casks (most of them, ironically, from Glaser's former employer).

To add to your pleasure they are superbly packaged, with elegant typography on witty and distinctive labels. Not cheap but immensely satisfying, any Compass Box whisky will mark you out as a drinker of taste and discernment. Asyla uses just four whiskies in the blend (single malts from Linkwood, Glen Elgin and Teaninich, and grain whisky from Cameron Bridge), but marries them for up to 12 months to create a sweet, delicate aperitif whisky that has rightly won huge plaudits.

Colour A pale golden whisky, set off by the elegant, tall, clear glass bottle.
Nose Apple, vanilla and some cereal notes. Grassy.
Taste This is sweet but not cloying; delicate and very subtle with great complexity. Like all Compass Box whiskies it is exceptionally smooth.
Finish Slightly drying. Some hints of smoke may be detected.

Verdict

8

Producer	Morrison Bowmore Distillers
Distillery	Auchentoshan, Dalmuir, nr Glasgow
Visitor Centre	Yes
Availability	Widespread international availability
Price	□□□□□

www.auchentoshan.co.uk

Auchentoshan

Classic

It seems only right to include one example of distilling in the true, traditional Lowland style – that is to say, triple distilled, like Irish whiskey. Auchentoshan is also a showpiece distillery, beautifully maintained by its owners Morrison Bowmore (a subsidiary of the Japanese group Suntory) and thus always a pleasure to visit.

The distillery was established round 1817 in open countryside, since which time residential development has surrounded the plant and it now appears a curious anachronism in an apparently urban setting close to the dramatic Erskine Bridge over the River Clyde. The owners have capitalised on this location by opening not just a visitor centre but also providing conference facilities for the business market.

The range of whiskies has been greatly increased in recent years and a number of different expressions, right up to 50 years old, are offered. It is light and delicate in style but, surprisingly, stands up well to cask finishing when this is handled with due sensitivity – the Three Wood is a fine example of what can be done and Auchentoshan seems to age quite gracefully. Presumably this reflects shrewd cask selection by the previous owners and continued investment by Suntory.

The result of Auchentoshan's triple distilling process is a smooth and very clean spirit that finishes life at over 80% abv, unusually high for the output of a pot still. There is an admirably clear animated diagram illustrating this on the excellent website – itself a model of clarity and unfussy operation.

If you don't know this whisky, then I suggest you start with the signature Classic. It's non-aged and the soft, creamy style will win friends easily. If you don't care for it, or find that you want more body, don't despair – its gentle style makes an excellent base for whisky cocktails, providing grip without dominating the desired flavour.

Colour   Pale and delicate – bottled quite young and matured in refill ex-bourbon, this hasn't picked up much colour.

Nose   Loads of vanilla; fresh and grassy.

Taste   Malty, plenty of marzipan sweetness cut with lemon zest and green apples.

Finish   Fresh and floral, but doesn't linger.

Verdict

Producer	Inver House Distillers Ltd
Distillery	Balblair, Edderton, Ross-shire
Visitor Centre	None
Availability	Specialists
Price	☐☐■☐☐

www.balblair.com

Balblair
Vintage 1989

Balblair is just along the road from its much better-known neighbour Glenmorangie (see separate entry) but maintains an altogether lower profile, perhaps rather grudgingly. The distillery is one of a clutch owned and resurrected by the Airdrie-based Inver House Distillers, themselves a subsidiary of the Thai conglomerate InterBev, who seem to specialise in taking other companies' unloved orphan children and making something of them.

It is one of the oldest distilleries still in existence in Scotland, dating back to 1790, though there are records of distilling on the site as far back as 1749. It was rebuilt in the 1870s by the owners, the Ross family (four out of the nine Balblair distillery workers still have the surname Ross), and appears to have changed relatively little since then, although it was shut from 1915 to 1947. Inver House aren't easily persuaded of the merits of change and tend to adhere to traditional methods where they can. Good for them.

What is not particularly traditional is the decision to release a series of vintage expressions, rather than the more normal aged variants. However, vintages have worked very well for The Glenrothes and there is some merit in the argument that spirit character does vary from year to year. It all adds variety to our shelves and has definitely worked in sales terms.

The Balblair 1989 vintage was a Gold Medal winner in the 2007 International Wine & Spirits Competition (IWSC) and judged 'best in class', and was a big favourite of the crowd at the 2008 Edinburgh Whisky Fringe (great event, try to get a ticket). For me, it represents an optimum compromise between availability, price and quality: it shows off the distillery style well, yet remains affordable and immensely quaffable.

Colour Pale amber, mainly from ex-bourbon casks.
Nose Aromas of raisin, green apple and hints of banana and coconut.
Taste Initially slightly harsh but rapidly evolves and warms, with spice, lemon, raisin and suggestions of nutty oak.
Finish Some dried fruit, but finishes quite quickly. Hints of smoke and a marine note.

Verdict

10

Producer Chivas Brothers Ltd
Distillery n/a – this is a blend
Visitor Centre n/a
Availability Specialists
Price ☐☐☐☐☐

Aged **17** Years

Ballantine's

FULLY MATURED · QUALITY GUARANTEED
ESTᵈ 1827

VERY OLD
SCOTCH WHISKY

17 YEARS OLD

BLENDED & BOTTLED BY
GEORGE BALLANTINE AND SON LTD
DISTILLERS DUMBARTON SCOTLAND
PRODUCT OF SCOTLAND

70cl   *Geo Ballantine*   43% vol

www.ballantines.com

Ballantine's
17 Years Old

This is a whisky with a considerable and distinguished pedigree, largely unappreciated in its home market. This, for a brand that markets itself with the slogan 'leave an impression', is more than slightly ironic. It's because this is a premium blend which, by and large, is a style that the UK market doesn't 'get'. Not that owners, Chivas Brothers, will be especially bothered because Ballantine's is huge in the Far East and in tax free (airports, to you and me).

The name is an honoured one. The original George Ballantine was one of the giants of Victorian whisky blending, starting from modest premises in Edinburgh in 1827 but, less than 60 years later, exporting around the world with a string of royal warrants to his name. However, as is the way of the spirits industry, the brand changed hands several times before Chivas Brothers acquired it in July 2005.

Between their astute marketing and the skills of their renowned Master Blender, Sandy Hyslop, Ballantine's has come roaring back. Fortunately, Hyslop has a very fine range of both grain and single malt whiskies from which to pick, and the experience and judgement to know how to put them together.

Probably the pick of the bunch is the 17 Years Old. It is pleasant, smooth, warming and mellow. There's plenty of depth there, but this does not assert itself forcefully; rather it slowly charms you until you realise what a very special dram it is. Talented but self-effacing and modest with it: the archetypal upper-middle-class Edinburgh professional, then. It does leave an impression, after all.

Colour Bright gold.
Nose Rounded, balanced and appetising. Some sweet notes and a hint of smoke.
Taste Mellow vanilla tones, with maturity showing in balanced wood, smoke and cream. Surprisingly full bodied for 43% abv and after chill filtration.
Finish Lingers agreeably at the back of the palate, holding together well and leaving hints of marine character.

Verdict

11

Producer	Beam Global Spirits & Wine, Inc.
Distillery	Jim Beam, Clermont Distillery, Kentucky
Visitor Centre	Yes
Availability	Specialists and online
Price	☐☐☐☐☐

www.smallbatch.com

Basil Hayden's

It's claimed that the Hayden family can be traced back to the years following the Norman Conquest of 1066. One ancestor, Simon de Heydon, was knighted by Richard the Lionheart in the Holy Land during the Third Crusade in the 1190s and his son, Thomas de Heydon, made Justice Itinerant of Norfolk by Henry III. Later, another ancestor was granted a large estate in Hertfordshire, in return for the family's military service. Eventually, however, they emigrated to the Virginia Colony in the 1660s in search of religious freedom.

It is further claimed that, by 1796, one Basil Hayden was a master distiller, born and raised in Maryland, where he learned to make whiskey from rye. Moving to Kentucky, Hayden began making whiskey from a base of corn, but added a higher percentage of rye than other distillers, resulting in smooth, mild bourbon. Well, that's the story anyway.

One of the Beam Small Batch bourbons, Basil Hayden's is unique in that it utilises twice as much rye (30%) as other small batch releases (though Beam adopt a similar approach to the distillation of their Old Grand-Dad). Unusually for premium bourbon, it is bottled at 40% abv, typically at around eight years of age, and is the lightest in style in the collection.

It always seems somewhat over-packaged for my taste with a tall and rather feminine bottle strangely bisected by a copper band, but if you like a dry and more delicate taste in your bourbon then this will appeal. It's also an excellent cocktail base.

Like all the Small Batch range, this comes from the large and rather utilitarian Clermont distillery, somewhat the antithesis of the small batch philosophy, but where you can at least visit the T. Jeremiah Beam Home and the Jim Beam American Outpost and try a range of products.

Colour Pale gold.
Nose Some citrus notes with mint and spice.
Taste Light to medium body, delicate and aromatic. Honey, pepper and fading spice.
Finish Quite short but holds together.

Verdict

12

Producer	The BenRiach Distillery Company Ltd
Distillery	BenRiach, Elgin, Morayshire
Visitor Centre	None – try phoning for an appointment
Availability	Specialists
Price	⬜⬛⬜⬜⬜

www.benriachdistillery.co.uk

BenRiach
Curiositas Peated

Bored of whiskies with strange Gaelic names? Why not try one with some Latin part of a range that includes Heredotus Fumossus and Importanticus Fumosus? You just have to be curious about 'Curiositas'. (It's an experimental, heavily peated Speysider.)

The names may seem a bit contrived, but here is a small independent distiller getting on with life, experimenting with unusual whiskies and managing to do so without developing a persecution complex.

BenRiach (I have no idea why they stick a capital letter in the middle) was lying mothballed from around 1900 until it was rebuilt and reopened sixty-five years later. It's a miracle it survived, but it only carried on until August 2002 when it was mothballed again.

However, at that point its luck changed. Having been owned by a series of large corporations, BenRiach was lucky to be acquired by industry veteran Billy Walker, backed by two South African investors. They have invested heavily in the distillery and, in August 2008, bought Glendronach as well, so things are obviously going swimmingly.

Sadly, there's no visitor centre (there is an excellent one at Glendronach) but it would be worth asking nicely for a peek, especially as they maintain a showpiece floor malting (sadly it's not currently in use).

There are a number of releases, some quite limited, and exciting plans. The distillery themselves say that their vision is 'not only to maintain the great traditions of the distillery but to break new ground with "new" whisky expressions and, borrowing from the wider world of the noble art of distilling, to "craft" special whiskies, and intriguing expressions'. It sounds exciting. It is exciting. And, hoping that the corporate giants don't swamp them, my toast to BenRiach is, *'nil carborundum illegitimi!'*

Colour Pale gold.
Nose Peat on this one, but not as aggressive as often found on Islay. Heather flowers in background.
Taste Medium weight, lots of peat attack, wood follows on with a spicy fruitiness.
Finish Plenty of that peat smoke but lots more going on to tease you *a capite ad calcem* *.

Verdict

* *'From head to heel", since you had to ask. Were you asleep in Double Latin?*

13

Producer	Gordon & MacPhail
Distillery	Benromach, Forres, Morayshire
Visitor Centre	Yes
Availability	Specialists
Price	

www.benromach.com

Benromach
Organic

There are a number of 'organic' whiskies out there – Da Mhile (first made at Springbank but now Loch Lomond); Highland Harvest blended and Bruichladdich will soon launch the first Islay Organic whisky, distilled in December 2003 and now approaching full maturity.

Personally, I can't see that it matters all that much in a distilled spirit but, if you care about these things, you will be interested in this offering from Benromach, Gordon & MacPhail's tiny distillery on the outskirts of Forres. So far as I can see, it's the first and so far the only whisky where the whole process – raw ingredients, distillation, maturation, bottling – is certified to the Soil Association's rigorous organic standards.

This does, however, add something of interest to the whisky enthusiast. For one thing the barley used for malting comes from a Scottish farm (not all barley used to make Scotch is Scottish, which may come as something of a surprise) and the barrels are from virgin oak. This is unusual – it's generally held that brand new oak barrels exert too assertive an influence on the flavour of Scotch whisky, hence the almost universal presence of barrels that have been seasoned by previous use. However, Benromach appear to have carried this off and, while clearly evident, the wood does not dominate.

The distillers claim that the casks are 'hand selected' – a nice-sounding but, as far as I can see, essentially meaningless claim since so far as I am aware, no one has yet invented a machine to select casks – and made from natural, wild-growing forest. The trees are not sprayed with pesticides or any other form of chemical prior to felling (but then they wouldn't, being 'wild') or indeed after.

Quite how you square your green concerns with the felling of natural wild forest is a matter for your own conscience, of course. You'll probably drink this while reading the *Guardian*.

Colour Rich, deep gold.
Nose Lots of wood impact, of course, but fruits and vanilla pods.
Taste Wood we take for granted here, but fruit compote and some sweetness also evident.
Finish A glow of liberal, green-tinted virtue.
Verdict

14

Producer	Heaven Hill Distilleries, Inc.
Distillery	Bernheim, Louisville, Kentucky
Visitor Centre	Yes
Availability	Specialists
Price	▪▪▪☐☐

www.bernheimwheatwhiskey.com see also www.heaven-hill.com

Bernheim

Original Wheat Whiskey

'Unique' and 'original' are grossly over-used terms, though I think probably justified here. This American whiskey is made with winter wheat as its principal ingredient (a minimum of 51%) along with the more conventional rye, barley and corn. As such, it is the first really new American whiskey since Prohibition and is arguably reviving a distilling style from the 1700s. Naturally, as the world's only straight wheat whiskey, it has attracted a lot of attention from enthusiasts anxious for a new taste sensation. At the time of writing it is the only example of this style, though presumably, if its success continues, we'll see other distillers offering something similar in the near future.

The distillery itself has had an interesting history. It was built on the site of the old Astor and Belmont distilleries, which were demolished by United Distillers, the forerunner of Diageo, before the brand new Bernheim plant was constructed in 1992. Under Diageo bourbon was not regarded as a priority and, in 1999, the Heaven Hill Company acquired the facility, which today makes it the last privately owned distillery in Kentucky. Among other brands, Heaven Hill Bourbon and Rittenhouse Rye is distilled here, all of which can be seen in the fine new Bourbon Heritage Centre, *Whisky Magazine*'s 2009 Visitor Attraction of the Year (there is a $50 'behind the scenes' tour). Bernheim Original is distilled here but aged for a minimum of two years in new charred white oak barrels in Rickhouse Y at Heaven Hill's site at Bardstown, Nelson County.

Launched in 2005 Bernheim Original Wheat Whiskey has benefited from interest in small batch production and craft distillation. As an innovative salute to tradition it is interesting but the whiskey itself holds up well.

Colour Pale, especially by comparison to bourbon.
Nose A delicate nose offers buttered toast, spices and some fruits. Clean and refreshing lemon zest.
Taste Fruit and nut. Medium bodied; sweet but not cloying.
Finish Crisp and spicy. Hints of nuts.

Verdict

15	Producer	Burn Stewart Distillers Ltd
	Distillery	n/a – this is a blend
	Visitor Centre	n/a
	Availability	Widespread international availability
	Price	□□□□□

A whole bottle in one night
9/5/08

www.blackbottle.com

Black Bottle

I was really hoping to write about Black Bottle's 10-year-old brother. This was launched in 1998 but, sadly, has been withdrawn, lasting as a brand only slightly longer than the whisky in the bottle. However, if you're really quick you might find the odd bottle on a dusty shelf somewhere. If so, grab it without hesitation, especially if you like the peaty stuff.

The standard style is more than respectable, however. It's one of those classic Victorian blends that started life in a grocer's shop, in this case in Aberdeen, and went on to change the fortunes of the family firm, Gordon Graham & Co. And, as is the way of these stories, eventually the family had to sell up and the brand went through a series of changes, some less than successful.

Eventually it ended up owned by Burn Stewart Distillers who, without lavishing money on it, have given it at least some of the tender loving care it cried out for. They have treated it with appropriate respect and improved the quality (actually, that's a recurring comment on a number of their whiskies generally – see Deanston and Tobermory, in particular).

Apparently, in its earliest days, each bottle was wrapped in tissue paper which carried this verse, generally attributed to Walter Landor:

If upon my theme I rightly think,
There are five reasons why I drink:
Good wine. A friend. Because I'm dry.
Because I might be bye and bye.
Or any other reason why!

Why you might want to drink Black Bottle is to enjoy a big, smoky, Islay-dominated blend (there's a bit of Deanston in there also, but it's rather swamped by the peat) that is rather more refreshing and easier to drink than many other peat-dominated drams. It's not expensive either, making it a good everyday standby.

Colour Pale, bright gold.

Nose Surprisingly light, fresh and fruity with peat in the background.

Taste Well balanced with a delightful sweetness acting as a kind of smoke extractor!

Finish The peat notes start to come through at the end as the whisky dies away; more embers than smoke.

Verdict

16

Producer	Highland Distillers
Distillery	n/a – this is a blend
Visitor Centre	The Famous Grouse Experience at Glenturret, near Crieff
Availability	Widespread international availability
Price	☐☐☐☐☐

www.thefamousgrouse.com see also www.black-grouse.com

Black Grouse

There seems precious little point in telling anyone about The Famous Grouse, as it has long been established as Scotland's best-selling blended Scotch, supported by those vaguely annoying but actually mildly amusing TV commercials with the ear-worm of a tune – so I won't. If desperate, you can learn more at their website (I find it rather tiresome and contrived; might just be me) or even visit The Famous Grouse Experience at Glenturret distillery near Crieff, essentially an over-blown visitor centre, shop and several restaurants, and try to find the tiny distillery somewhere in the middle of it all.

But something has been stirring in the nest in recent years and the grouse has brought forth a clutch of interesting new fledglings with some discreet test marketing going on as they try to stretch the brand. Two that have successfully flown the nest (sorry, that's the last tedious pun) are the Snow Grouse, a harshly chill-filtered blended grain, about which the less said the better, and the Black Grouse.

It's curious that it should follow immediately on from Black Bottle, because this is another Islay-influenced, peaty blend. Ironic, then, you may think, that Highland Distillers sold their only Islay distillery (Bunnahabhain) in 2003 (not that it was particularly noted for peated whiskies at that time anyway).

Anyway, noting the fashion for smoky whiskies, the blenders have fashioned this smooth and aromatic drop, which seems to be finding favour among peat freaks, not least for its competitive pricing. The Famous Grouse pack (or covey) appears to number nine and counting now, though I daresay more will have hatched by the time this gets into print (sorry, I didn't even try to resist it).

Colour A mature, rich, coppery gold.
Nose Smoky and spicy but not assertive or harsh.
Taste Pleasantly well-balanced, smooth and mouth coating; some signature Grouse sweetness but develops spice and fruit character as Speyside and Islay merge.
Finish Cocoa and spices but with a fading smoke character.

Verdict

17

Producer	Co-ordinated Development Services Ltd
Distillery	Bladnoch, Wigtown, Kirkcudbrightshire
Visitor Centre	Yes
Availability	Specialists
Price	☐■☐☐☐

www.bladnoch.co.uk

Bladnoch

8 Years Old

Is this the best whisky in this book? Probably not, but you should still buy a bottle – and here's why.

Bladnoch, one of the very last Lowland distilleries and Scotland's most southerly distillery, was closed in June 1993 by UDV (now Diageo). An Irish builder and property developer, Raymond Armstrong, bought the site.

Unlikely as it now seems, he planned to redevelop the buildings for housing. But the whisky gods were not to be so easily distracted and, after some time, Armstrong began to understand what the distillery meant to the local community. So he determined to start distilling again.

That wasn't quite as easy as it sounds and UDV, who had sold on the strict understanding that Bladnoch was to be taken out of production, took some persuading to permit even limited distilling. But, at the risk of racial stereotyping, Armstrong has the blarney and is both persistent and charming. Eventually he got them to relent and, in December 2000, Bladnoch went back into production.

For this he attained the rank of whisky hero and is revered among aficionados. He is also a thoroughly amenable and agreeable fellow, happy to pass the time of day with you if you drop in, and an all-round good egg. Today, the site is pleasantly busy, has a charming home-spun visitor centre and they run an open-spirited and generous discussion forum on their website.

The first whisky distilled under Armstrong's benevolent and affable ownership was released in October 2009 at the Wigtown Book Festival. Buy a bottle and help keep a dream alive: it's a noble and worthy cause. Every bottle sold helps.

Colour Pale straw.
Nose Lemon zest, oak and vanilla. Slightly spirity but with nutty suggestions.
Taste Light to medium body, but mouth coating. Loads of vanilla and crème brûlée flavours.
Finish Not the longest finish ever, light with some spice notes. Just buy it anyway.

Verdict

18

Producer
Distillery
Visitor Centre

Availability
Price

Berry Bros & Rudd
n/a – this is a blend
No – but visit their
London shop
Specialists
■■■□□

PRODUCT OF SCOTLAND

4th
LIMITED RELEASE
SCOTS WHISKY

BOTTLED 2008

BLENDED MALT SCOTS WHISKY
NATURAL COLOUR & NON - CHILLFILTERED

70cl   45.6%vol

BLUE HANGER

BERRY BROS & RUDD

3 ST JAMES'S STREET, LONDON SW1, UK

www.bbr.com

Blue Hanger

Top people's wine merchants Berry Bros & Rudd, with their elegant premises in London's St James's Street, is not the first place you'd go to find a bargain. But there is one lurking there. Remember, while you might associate them with classed growth claret, these are the folks who created Cutty Sark so they do know their whisky.

This little cracker is what's known as a blended malt; that is to say, a blend (or mixture) of several single malts with no grain whisky at all allowed to the party. Berry's whisky guy is the highly regarded Doug McIvor. You know all you need to know about Doug when I tell you that of all the blenders in the Scotch whisky industry he was the one entrusted with the samples from the late Michael Jackson's* whisky library to create a memorial blend.

For this fourth release, Doug has combined three Speyside malts: Glen Elgin, Glenlivet and Mortlach, ranging from 16 to 34 years old. He himself describes the whisky as having 'a strong influence from Sherry casks but I try to rein this in to offer balance and complexity from the other casks'. That's a little modest: the previous release of Blue Hanger was a comfortable winner in the blended malt class in the 2008 World Whiskies Awards and it's generally agreed that with this fourth release he has surpassed even that high standard. What's more agreeable is that it's bottled at 45.6% and you will pay around £60 for a bottle. Just pray they don't decide to put it in some lavish packaging.

The unusual name comes from William Hanger, 3rd Lord Coleraine, a loyal customer of Berry's during the 18th century. He was renowned for wearing striking blue clothes, and gained the sobriquet 'Blue Hanger'. You don't have to dress up to shop there, but I told you they were posh.

Colour Dark – age and sherry casks showing here.
Nose Rich and promising; stewed fruits and some suggestion of citrus.
Taste Leather, vanilla and stewed pear hints developing to cream fudge and rich orange. Full bodied.
Finish Dry, with hints of smoke and nuts.

Verdict

* No, not the American singer. Try and keep up – this is a whisky book!

49

19

Producer	Glenmorangie plc
Distillery	n/a – this is a blend
Visitor Centre	n/a
Availability	Specialists
Price	☐☐☐☐☐

BNJ

Bailie Nicol Jarvie

What's this doing here? You may well ask, since it seems to me that the owners clearly don't care. Bailie Nicol Jarvie ('BNJ' to its coterie of dedicated fans) appears to be the unloved and, it would seem, unwanted runt of the litter in the Glenmorangie stable. But they haven't killed it off with neglect and disinterest, nor have they managed to sell it to someone who would lavish on it the tender loving care that it so evidently deserves (though, as we go to print, there are unconfirmed rumours that it's being offered for sale, so it may be in new hands by the time you read this).

The blend has been around for years (I have seen a very lovely pre-war decanter in a Highland shooting lodge – really this whisky's natural habitat) and is reputed to contain an uncommonly high percentage of single malt whisky, most probably Glenmorangie and Glen Moray. The result is a subtle and complex, though relatively light-bodied, blend that has quietly attracted admirers among informed drinkers.

It's entirely irrelevant but it also has a great label. Just thought I'd mention it, as it marks you out as a drinker of taste and discernment, capable of looking beyond ritzy packaging to timeless elegance. More importantly, it is fantastic value.

That might explain the owners' reluctance to push sales: with this much top-quality single malt in the blend the price is simply too low if it becomes a success, especially given the cost of building a brand. So get in fast. Fill yer boots. This can't last and you need to get some while you still can.

Colour	Pale and interesting.
Nose	Fresh and floral, with the Glenmorangie influence evident. Pears and grassy notes – very elegant.
Taste	A very well-balanced, well-mannered whisky. Just a hint of smoke covering delicate perfumed notes; fresh fruit and hazelnuts.
Finish	Subtle and delicate. A rapier of a whisky but with a killer edge of spice, chocolate and toffee.

Verdict

20

Producer Morrison Bowmore Distillers
Distillery Bowmore, Islay
Visitor Centre Yes
Availability Specialists
Price ☐☐■☐☐

www.bowmore.co.uk

Bowmore

Tempest

Islay's oldest distillery (founded in 1779, or possibly even earlier) retains a floor malting which produces around one third of the malted barley required by the operation. You can take a tour which includes the malting floor and you may be permitted to look into the kiln with its haircloth floor (the perforated metal sheet onto which the grain is spread to be dried). Even with no fire underneath, the whole place retains the richly aromatic, almost pungent, smell of peat smoke.

And that, of course, is what Islay is really all about and what makes the whiskies so special. For my money, Bowmore is one of the better balanced drams produced here and the peat content (measured in parts per million of phenols) is a little lower than some of its more assertive neighbours. Not that this should make you make the mistake of thinking any less of it. This is very fine whisky and is highly sought after – rare and old expressions of Bowmore are one of the most valuable of whisky collectables and feature regularly in whisky auctions. Indeed, an 1850 bottling sold in September 2007 for a then world-record price of £29,400, though not without attracting some controversy and speculation as to its authenticity. Presumably the buyer was happy.

However, you can pick up a bottle of their Tempest – a tasty, cask strength, non-chill filtered, 10-year-old Bowmore for around £40, which makes it something of a bargain. It'll never be worth £29,000 but that's not the point. This is one to drink and savour, and is probably my current favourite from an extensive and impressive range that has enjoyed deserved success in recent years.

Try, if you can, to get to the distillery. The tour is well managed and the bar at the visitor centre offers a stunning view over Loch Indaal, which is capable of soothing the soul of even the most stressed-out urban sophisticate.

Colour	Bright gold.
Nose	Peat smoke and salt, hints of orange crème brûlée and honey.
Taste	The signature subtle Bowmore peat smoke to the fore, with salt and a playful citrus note.
Finish	A maritime farewell, peat smoke over a stormy sea, but clean and fresh.

Verdict

21

Producer	Bruichladdich Distillery Company
Distillery	Bruichladdich, Islay
Visitor Centre	Yes
Availability	Specialists and some supermarkets
Price	☐■☐☐☐

www.bruichladdich.com

Bruichladdich
12 Years Old Second Edition

I spent a long time pondering over whether or not to include Bruichladdich and eventually decided that, despite what you're about to read, I love them really. Try to keep that in mind!

Mind you, they do make it hard. If it's not the preposterous claims on their website ('pre-industrial distilling techniques' indeed? From a distillery built in 1881...), or what seems to this commentator at least a persistently chippy attitude and obsessive belief that everyone is out to do them down, then it must be the tediously self-aggrandising claims (apparently, they are 'The Malt Crusaders: fiercely independent, non-conformist, innovative – the enfant terrible of the industry'). In fact, they're in danger of becoming the Millwall fans of whisky ('no one likes us, we don't care').

Actually, despite the waves of sycophantic publicity – at least one rather obsequious book, regular TV appearances and a documentary has been broadcast about them (publicity that the average marketing manager would kill for) – the truth is that no one's that bothered by their antics. If only they would concentrate on making whisky since they do it so very, very well.

But the difficulty here is finding one to pick. Bruichladdich are (in)famous for a never-ending series of releases and finishes (except in Bruichladdich-speak they're not 'finishes', so now I'll be in even more trouble) that roll off Islay with mind-numbing frequency. There is a sort of strange logic, but it relies on having a very Bruichladdich-centric world view to appreciate it.

Anyway, just to be clear: the distillery is a wonderful time capsule; the people are passionate; they make wonderful whisky and aren't afraid to try new things; and they have brought a lot of heat (and some light) to the Scotch whisky scene. So start off with the 12 Years Old, which is as near as you will get to a standard expression. Expensive by comparison with other malts of a similar age, but what do you expect from renegades?

Colour Bright gold.
Nose Lots going on: refined, floral, fruity and subtle.
Taste Fairly light bodied but not without interest. Starts sweet, fruit develops, then vanilla and oak.
Finish Fades gently away with the fruit notes drying as it ends.

Verdict

22

Producer	The Sazerac Company
Distillery	Buffalo Trace, Franklin County, Kentucky
Visitor Centre	Yes
Availability	Specialists
Price	☐☐☐☐☐

www.buffalotrace.com see also **www.bourbonwhiskey.com**

Buffalo Trace

An outstanding and highly-awarded distiller of Kentucky Straight Bourbon, the Buffalo Trace distillery was founded in 1857, though there was distilling on the site some seventy years earlier. Buffalo Trace has the distinction of being the first producer of single barrel bourbon with the 1984 release of Blanton's.

A number of brands are produced here as well as Buffalo Trace: Eagle Rare, Blanton's, Rock Hill Farms, Hancock's, Elmer T. Lee, Sazerac Rye and W.L. Weller, among others. But it is the distillery's own label that we're concerned with, first introduced in 1999. It found rapid acceptance and acclaim. Today they can boast on their website that 'the distillery has won more international awards since 1990 than any other North American distillery, earning more than 140 distinctions in national and international competitions'.

At the heart of it is this fine example of Kentucky Straight Bourbon. The distillers believe that certain floors of some of their warehouses (romantically, they are named as warehouses C, I and K) produce the best spirit, and small batches of the best casks are selected for Buffalo Trace. These go through a further selection by a taste panel and as few as 25 barrels are then married and bottled.

Interestingly, the three warehouses share similar construction: they are rick warehouses constructed from large wood beams and surrounded by a brick shell. Each has an earth floor (like a dunnage warehouse in Scotland) and, during the winter, steam is pumped throughout the warehouses to compensate for the dramatic drop in temperature. This has the effect of forcing the whiskey to mature faster – which is just great because it gets to us that little bit quicker!

Buffalo Trace is well distributed in good specialists in the UK. I'd say it was the perfect introduction to bourbon, after which other brands at this price point will disappoint.

Colour Light bronze. No added colour.
Nose Vanilla, mint, spice and some citrus hints.
Taste Sweet with vanilla, cinnamon, brown sugar and oak wood.
Finish Quite long and drying.

Verdict

Producer
Distillery
Visitor Centre

Availability
Price

Burn Stewart Distillers Ltd
Bunnahabhain, Islay
Yes – modest facilities at
the distillery
Specialists
◻◻◻◻◻◻

www.bunnahabhain.com

Bunnahabhain

18 Years Old

I am inordinately fond of Bunnahabhain. I once spent a wonderful holiday there (you can rent one of the former distillery cottages) and it is one of the quietest and most relaxing places that you'll ever find.

The distillery itself is more functional than picturesque but it lies at the heart of a pretty bay, with exceptional views over the Sound of Jura. Since I spent time there, Bunnahabhain has been sold to Burn Stewart, a small Scotch whisky distilling company ultimately owned in Trinidad, and this has been a thoroughly good thing.

Previously, it was rather dwarfed by its glamorous stable mates, The Macallan and Highland Park. Now it may be in a smaller pond, but it's a bigger fish and all the more comfortable for that. The established distilling team largely stayed intact but an injection of TLC followed the transfer of ownership and some interesting whiskies were quickly prised out of the warehouses.

Where once there was only a somewhat anodyne 12-year-old version, today there are several aged expressions and occasional – and usually interesting and rewarding – special editions. Recommended here for its blend of quality and value is the 18-year-old style. This is not heavily peated, though the distillery is experimenting with this style. If you like peat, look out for what they call their Mòine or Toiteach styles (hard to find, though).

If you ever get to Islay it's easy to forget about Bunnahabhain, which lies somewhat out of the way. That would be a mistake: it's well worth a visit.

Colour Bright, rich gold.
Nose Hints of honey and nuts; soft, elegant, with mild aromas of sherry.
Taste Caramel toffee, old leather and oak. A salt influence may be detected, with mint and sweet spice.
Finish Well balanced, drying, with sherry and spice notes. Slight hints of fading smoke.

Verdict

24

Producer	Diageo
Distillery	Bushmills, Co. Antrim, Northern Ireland
Visitor Centre	Yes
Availability	Specialists
Price	▪▪▪□□

www.bushmills.com

Bushmills

16 Years Old

Does it actually matter when a distillery was founded? I mean, if you thought that Bushmills dated from, say, 1784 rather than, say, 1608 would you buy any less? The distillery makes great play of the earlier date, emphasising it on their bottles and labels, while being rather coy about the fact that this relates to a generic licence to distil in their general area and that the Bushmills trademark doesn't first appear until 176 years later. Well, what's a century or two among friends? After all, their competitors have all disappeared and 1784 was a very long time ago (it marked the formal end of the American War of Independence, for one thing). To be fair, the website does clear up the 1608 thing, so we'll let them off.

Bushmills, now part of the Diageo stable, is Northern Ireland's last surviving distillery – and a large and successful one it is at that. Having survived a huge fire, Prohibition, a vigorous temperance movement and competition from Scotch whisky, Bushmills has entered its fifth (or possibly third, depending on the above) century in great shape.

The standard Bushmills and the slightly premium Black Bush are both blends (curiously, the grain whisky comes from the Republic where it's made at Midleton, by their great competitor) but the distillery offers three 100% malted barley single malts, at 10, 16 and 21 years of age.

There is an excellent visitor centre at the distillery and, by taking the tour, you can see triple distillation in action. From the Bushmills range, I've selected the 16 Years Old single malt. The extra age and up to a year's finishing in port wood add colour and depth of flavour to what is already very fine spirit. The 21 Years Old is much harder to find and significantly more expensive.

Colour The attractive ruby red tint is a clear signal of port finishing.

Nose Waves of fruit on the nose, immediately appealing sweet notes and some wood gets through.

Taste More fruit, but also malty caramel toffee and some chocolate. Medium to full bodied.

Finish Sinuous waves of complexity – a reminder of all the flavours in the glass – fading delightfully slowly.

Verdict

25

Producer	Diageo
Distillery	Cameron Bridge, Fife
Visitor Centre	None
Availability	Specialists
Price	☐☐☐☐☐

Cameron Brig

This is grain whisky – Scotland's equivalent of the mad aunt in the attic who no one talks about. But the Scotch whisky industry absolutely depends on it because it is at the basis of blending. If there was no grain whisky there would be no Johnnie Walker, no Famous Grouse, no Ballantine's and so on – and far fewer single malts, too, as almost all single malt distilleries rely on blended whiskies to take the majority of their output.

So why so coy? Well, grain whisky is produced on an industrial scale by a somewhat different process than single malt, using cheaper ingredients. Generally speaking, grain distilleries aren't pretty and they don't conform to the image that the industry likes to sell us. What's more, most grain whisky is used within a few months of its maturation and is valued more for its relatively bland flavour than any distinctive qualities (there are exceptions, of course, but this is broadly true).

However, a few grain whiskies are marketed in their own right and it's worth trying one or two just to expand your whisky education. Compass Box's excellent Hedonism is one (see separate entry) but it's hard to find and unusual in that it is blended grain. For a lot less money, track down a bottle of Cameron Brig. It won't be easy but it's worth the trouble.

If you don't care for it you can always try your hand at making your own blend. Take an empty bottle, fill it just over half full with the Cameron Brig and add a few of your favourite single malts. Shake well, say the magic words and, hey presto, you're a blender!

Colour Warm gold.
Nose Clean and grassy. Unpeated, so light and refreshing.
Taste Honey and spice. Warming and smooth (non-aged but presumably eight to ten years old).
Finish Subtle and surprisingly complex.

Verdict

26

Producer	Diageo
Distillery	Caol Ila, Islay
Visitor Centre	Yes
Availability	Specialists
Price	☐■☐☐☐

CAOL ILA

AGED **12** YEARS

ISLAY SINGLE MALT WHISKY

Deep aglt, in a remote cove near Port Askaig lies Caol Ila, hidden from among Islay's distilleries since 1846. Not easy to find, Caol Ila's secret malt is nonetheless highly prized among devotees of the Islay style.

Caol Ila Distillery, Port Askaig, Isle of Islay.

www.malts.com

Caol Ila
12 Years Old

It's great to be able to recommend whiskies like this – virtually unknown little secrets that, once tasted, are never forgotten. Caol Ila (pronounced 'cowl eela' – Gaelic speakers look away please) must be one of the most dramatically located of all of Scotland's distilleries. It's at the end of a precipitous road just outside Port Askaig on Islay, right on the sea, opposite the island of Jura. From the Manager's office window you can see seals, otters and all kinds of interesting sea birds, not to mention the amazing topography of Jura and the famous Paps (stop sniggering, they're great big hills).

But that's what not makes it so great. This is probably the unsung hero of Islay's renowned whiskies, largely because virtually all of the annual production is required for blending and the owners, Diageo, hardly promote the single malt. They do, however, grudgingly release some expressions – but these are generally quite pricy if you don't know you like them and are often restricted in availability anyway.

So why not start with the standard 12 Years Old? It's probably the best balanced of the Caol Ila expressions and a classic of its kind. In common with most Islay single malts it's for lovers of smoky whisky. Like its better-known neighbours at Lagavulin, Laphroaig and Ardbeg, it's a forceful, peat-soaked monster, but some drinkers find it a little sweeter than these.

There are some other versions, including an un-peated version (why bother?), but this is the one you're looking for. If you like this you can move on to its big brother at 18 Years Old and then try one of the many merchant bottlings that are out there. But this is the place to start.

Colour A light coloured whisky.

Nose The sweet malt hits one initially, followed by peat, treacle toffee and gentle lemon/citrus.

Taste Medicinal, but not aggressively so; wet grass, linseed oil and smoky wood. Add water to release sweet biscuits and more smoky, meaty notes.

Finish Peat smoke and lemon pudding battle it out to the end!

Verdict

27

Producer	Chivas Brothers Ltd
Distillery	n/a
Visitor Centre	n/a
Availability	Specialists and duty free
Price	⬜⬛⬜⬛⬛

www.chivas.com

Chivas Regal
25 Years Old

You get what you pay for, or so the saying goes. Here you pay rather a lot – typically around £180 in the UK, to be precise – around 4 to 5 times the price of its junior partner, the 18–year-old style. So what do you get? Apart from a very nice bottle, an extra heavyweight stopper and nice packaging, that is?

Using mainly Speyside single malts, with Strathisla at its heart, Chivas Regal 25 is the creation of Chivas Master Blender Colin Scott who describes it as 'the very pinnacle of the blend'. According to the company, the blend includes a proportion of vatted malts, which have been marrying in wood for what is described as 'a very long period of time'. Scott, widely respected in the industry, has been doing this for a very long period of time himself and has excelled himself here with the pick of the enviable Chivas malt warehouses.

A long-standing favourite luxury blend at 12 years old, Chivas Regal was initially launched by the original owners as a 25-year-old back in 1909 and was arguably the world's first super-premium whisky. Until this release, however, it had only recently been available at 12 and 18 years old. The 25 Years Old is smooth, sumptuous and very rich, with fruit and nut notes, hints of rich chocolate orange and a subtly smoky finish.

With a worldwide release of what is necessarily a limited quantity of whisky, initial stocks were targeted at markets such as the USA and the Far East but you can find this in good specialists. With its handsome presentation, it makes a wonderful and generous gift – if you can bear to part with it!

Colour   A rich, dark golden tone.
Nose   Orange and ripe peach; Christmas cake and nuts.
Taste   Rich and very full, the age showing clearly but with great vitality. Everything from the nose but more. And more besides.
Finish   Hints of smoke linger on in a well-balanced and well-mannered conclusion.

Verdict

28

Producer	Diageo
Distillery	Clynelish, Brora, Sutherland
Visitor Centre	Yes
Availability	Specialists and duty free
Price	☐■☐☐☐

BRORA · SUTHERLAND
CLYNELISH

Single Malt
CLYNELISH
COASTAL HIGHLAND
*Scotch
Whisky*

RESOLUTE INTEGRITY,
CONSISTENT QUALITY,
AND AN EXEMPLARY
STRENGTH OF CHARACTER

Years **14** Old

Distilled and Bottled in Scotland
CLYNELISH DISTILLERY
BRORA, SUTHERLAND
SCOTLAND

46% vol   70cl e

www.malts.com

Clynelish
14 Years Old

Two distinguished judges of whisky established Clynelish's reputation as a single whisky more than 80 years ago: both Professor George Saintsbury (in *Notes on a Cellar-Book*) and his student Aeneas MacDonald (*Whisky*) drew attention to its exceptional quality. Except, of course, that it was not the Clynelish that we drink now that they enjoyed, for the original distillery was actually closed in 1983. To sample anything resembling the spirit that they praise so highly you'll need to find several hundred pounds for a bottle of 30-year-old Brora.

When the owners decided to close the original 1819 distillery, they transfered the name to the new plant. But the old distillery was then reopened in 1967, mainly to produce heavily peated malt for blending, and both produced Clynelish until the Brora name was given to the original distillery in 1975. It was never intended that either should be sold as a single malt but the growing demand for single malts and the distillery's historic reputation persuaded the owners (by then Diageo) to release some limited expressions, which have been enthusiastically received.

Confused? If in doubt, check the price tag – you're looking for the more readily available and affordable Clynelish at 14 years old, which should cost less than £35 a bottle. If it's got a three-figure price tag, put it back – carefully.

This is what Diageo refer to as a 'Hidden Malt'. Not that they don't want you to find it at all, it just feels sometimes as if they're determined to make it difficult for you. Actually, they probably can't spare that much because it's a key component in the Johnnie Walker blends. It's better, though, to try the real thing: charming Highland malt with a maritime note from its seaside location.

Colour A bright mid-gold.
Nose Spicy and perfumed, with the signature 'candle wax' note loved by fans.
Taste At most medium bodied, but with a creamy/waxy mouth-coating impact. Floral, exotic fruit and spices, hints of smoke and honey.
Finish A salty, drying, slightly bitter finish.

Verdict

29

Producer	Diageo
Distillery	Gimli, Manitoba, Canada
Visitor Centre	Yes
Availability	Specialists and duty free
Price	■■□□□

www.crownroyal.com

Crown Royal

There are only two Canadian whiskies in this book; not because they aren't interesting but because, in general, they are hard to find in the UK and – let's be honest – we rather tend to look down on them. This, as we shall see, is our mistake.

Crown Royal is the number one Canadian whisky in the world, and the eighth largest spirits brand in the US – a position it hasn't reached entirely accidentally. It is also found in France, Japan and Korea where the somewhat lurid purple packaging of the velvet bag that it comes in and the regal associations are strongly associated with quality.

Not that the royal link is entirely a marketing creation. This dates to 1939 when the original blend was created to mark a visit to Canada by King George VI and Queen Elizabeth (later known to bookmakers the length and breadth of the land as the Queen Mother). This was in the days when Seagram owned the brand. Today it is in the hands of Diageo and has been produced since 1968 at the giant Gimli distillery, on the edge of Lake Winnipeg, built as something of a high watermark for the ultimately doomed Seagram Company. It's actually worth reading their history as a great example of mistimed decisions and corporate over-enthusiasm.

There are several expressions in the Crown Royal range including a Reserve, Cask No. 16 and the ultra-premium XR (you might just find these in duty free shops in North America). The standard expression has an enthusiastic following and it's a great ambassador for Canada. What's more, it's often found in the UK in 1 litre bottles, which offer great value.

It must be admitted that the bag is a bit of a problem, especially if you like to display your bottles. Don't let it put you off. Someone on eBay might want it. Somewhere a doll's house needs new curtains.

Colour Mid gold.
Nose Sweet initial impact; honey, spices and red berries. Oak and vanilla.
Taste Medium to full bodied, fruity with spice hints. Sweet and creamy.
Finish Vaguely pleasant and sweet, drifts slowly to a conclusion.

Verdict

30

Producer The Edrington Group
Distillery n/a – this is a blend
Visitor Centre n/a
Availability Mainly USA, Spain and Greece –
but fighting back in the UK

Price □□□□□

www.cutty-sark.com

Cutty Sark
Original

For a while this was the best-selling blended whisky in the USA, perhaps on the back of its availability during Prohibition. This was largely due to the efforts of noted bootlegger Captain William McCoy whose strenuous efforts to run only the best quality supplies ashore to his thirsty customers gave rise to the phrase 'the real McCoy'. Curiously, it was known originally as 'Scots' whisky.

But, unlike its rather vibrant yellow label, it has faded somewhat in recent years, which is a shame. Its extremely pale colour is out of fashion but there is still plenty to enjoy about this pleasant, light-bodied blend. For one thing, though for years it's been marketed by smart London wine merchants Berry Bros & Rudd, the whisky is actually blended by Highland Distillers and contains a healthy measure of great malts such as Glenrothes, The Macallan and Highland Park. In fact, Highland Park was actually bought by the blenders back in 1937 to ensure supplies for Cutty Sark, though it has gone on to great success in its own right (see separate entries). Earlier in 2010, Highland's parent, The Edrington Group, bought the brand from Berry Bros who had just relaunched it in the UK, so fans of this light and refreshing whisky can have high hopes for its future.

Until now, the main effort has been on the standard product, recommended here, but there is also a range of older styles available. You'll find Cutty mainly in London's smarter style bars and cocktail establishments and this is a hint about how to enjoy this whisky. Undemanding yet of excellent quality, Cutty Sark is the perfect pre-dinner dram and it also mixes well. Don't be fooled by the pale colour – there's more here than meets the eye.

Colour A very pale golden whisky, set off by the elegant, tall, clear glass bottle and striking yellow label.

Nose Vanilla and some cereal notes.

Taste Delicate and very subtle – a great aperitif whisky.

Finish Crisp and clean.

Verdict

31

Producer
Distillery
Visitor Centre
Availability

Price

The Edrington Group
n/a – this is a blend
n/a
Mainly USA, Spain and Greece –
but fighting back in the UK
◻◻◻◼◻

www.cutty-sark.com

Cutty Sark
25 Years Old

Blending was once defined by David MacDonald as 'The art of combining meticulously selected, mature, high quality whiskies, each with its own flavour and other characteristics, with such skill that the whole is better than the sum of its parts, so that each makes its contribution to the finished blend without any one predominating.'

It is an idealistic view, ignoring as it does the economic pressures behind many of the cheaper blends that we see on our shelves. Yet, at its best, this is what great blending is about and is a standard to which all distillers aspire, at least in their premium expressions. Once in a while, one comes across a whisky that brings that definition alive: this is such a whisky.

Savour it carefully: Cutty Sark 25 Years Old is a virtuoso display of blending excellence; exactly what blending is all about. I doubt you would ever tire of drinking this whisky. It is so smooth, so balanced, so refined, so perfectly tuned that even the most demanding critic would surely be satisfied and cry for more.

It comes as a surprise that it carries the Cutty Sark label, being as far removed from the standard blend as one might imagine. Where that is deliberately pale, this is dark; where that is clean and crisp, this is deep and rich. It carries its age very well, yet like great Stilton is clearly mature. Drinking it, I kept thinking of a vintage Bentley – progressing swiftly, purposefully and quietly, yet with a stately dignity and grace that only this rare combination of finesse and power can convey.

Let us name and honour the man behind this exceptional creation: John Ramsay, Master Blender at Edrington. Sir, we salute you! As he has recently retired, blending will fall to his successor, Gordon Motion. I hope he's kept some notes.

Colour Deep, dark and dignified.
Nose Marmalade, old oak and dark honey.
Taste Outstanding balance of power and subtlety. Rich fruit cake, Seville oranges and toffee.
Finish A long, rich and warm finish with some spice and faint smoke traces.

Verdict

32

Producer   Diageo
Distillery   Dalwhinnie, Dalwhinnie,
    Inverness-shire

Visitor Centre   Yes
Availability   Widespread international
    availability

Price   ☐■☐☐☐

www.malts.com

Dalwhinnie
15 Years Old

Dalwhinnie distillery lies just off the main A9, the arterial route from Edinburgh to Inverness and its shiny pagodas are clearly visible from the road. But try not to look, because this is one of the more dangerous sections of a dangerous road. Instead, turn off a mile or so to the south and spend an hour touring the distillery and looking at the small displays.

The owners, Diageo, lay much stress on the fact that the distillery is one of the highest in Scotland, though the precise significance of this escapes me. It is not as if lower atmospheric pressure will influence the whisky but it seems to have some romantic value in marketing. In fact, the reason for the remote location is rather more prosaic: the original distillery, then known as Strathspey, was put here to take advantage of the railway, a hugely significant influence on Victorian distillery construction, even if the spinmeisters would rather talk about water!

The distillers themselves claim that, 'Dalwhinnie is situated between the gentle, grassy style of the Lowlands and the austere, firm body of Speyside, which begins some 25 miles to the north. The style is that of the Highlands; a resilient marriage of gentleness and spirit.' That perhaps undersells the merits of this silky, mouth-coating spirit.

Interestingly, the distillery used to employ copper worm tubs to condense the new make. They were replaced in 1986 but the impact on spirit character was such that the change was reversed in 1995. So, fifteen years on, it's a moot point as to the effect on the current bottling but, such is the demand for the single malt expression in Diageo's Classic Malt Collection, supplies will probably have reverted to worm tub condensed spirit by the time you read this.

Colour Yellow gold.

Nose Immediately appealing; gentle smoke with honey, ripe fruits and grassy heather.

Taste Often said to appeal to those who 'don't like whisky', this is actually more complex than it first appears and offers hidden depths of vanilla with subtle orange suggestions.

Finish Some smoke surprises, then gives way to a sweeter finish. Perhaps dark chocolate also.

Verdict

33

Producer	Burn Stewart Distillers Ltd
Distillery	Deanston, Doune, Perthshire
Visitor Centre	No – tours by appointment
Availability	Specialists
Price	☐☐☐☐☐

✓

had a tester bottle

AGED **12** YEARS

DEANSTON

HIGHLAND SINGLE MALT
SCOTCH WHISKY

UN–CHILL FILTERED
(EXACTLY AS-IT SHOULD BE)

SIMPLE, HANDCRAFTED, NATURAL

www.burnstewartdistillers.com

Deanston

12 Years Old

It's not often recalled that Perthshire was once a major distilling centre, with over 100 distilleries recorded. Today there are still six in operation – Deanston is the one everyone but the most hard-core enthusiast will forget.

It makes it into this list as one of the most improved whiskies I can call to mind, coming from a distillery as interesting as it is obscure. But ignore any references to 1785. This is when the original building was erected but it was a cotton mill, designed by Richard Arkwright and powered by the fast-flowing River Neith. Today Arkwright's cellars, which are listed, provide ideal conditions for the maturation of whisky and the distillery is still powered by turbines driven by the Neith. In fact, the distillery generates more power than it needs – enough electricity to run 400 houses is sold to the National Grid.

The mill was converted to a full working distillery in 1966 and the first spirit ran in 1969 from two pairs of large bulbous pot stills, capable of distilling three million litres of alcohol a year. The large boiling balls on the stills encourage a high degree of reflux, leading to a light and fruity spirit character. The original intention was to use this in launching a major new blend, but this never happened.

Deanston was first released as single malt in 1974 and, by stages, was developed to a 12 Years Old product. But, to be blunt, it wasn't terribly good. Not bad; neither interesting nor memorable.

With the newly released version, however, things are looking up. The strength has been increased to 46.3% abv, it's not chill filtered any longer, it's married in new oak for some weeks prior to bottling and there's no added colour. It's a lot better and worth a try. Still quite light and delicate, but then you don't want some roaring peat-soaked monster or huge sherry character every day.

Colour Yellow gold.

Nose Fresh and fruity, with malt, hints of honey and nuts. Fragrant and quite floral.

Taste An ideal aperitif. Gingerbread, spices and liquorice.

Finish Long, quite dry and pleasantly herbal, with new wood notes at the back.

Verdict

34

Producer
Distillery
Visitor Centre

Availability

Price

John Dewar & Sons Ltd
n/a – this is a blend
Dewar's World of Whisky,
Aberfeldy, Perthshire
Strong in the USA, duty free
and Greece. Increasingly
available in the UK
☐☐☐☐☐

www.dewars.com

Dewar's

12 Years Old

The Dewar's company was bought by Bacardi in 1988 and the range of products greatly increased. Not that there was anything seriously wrong with the old White Label but the new blends have reached higher standards. One felt the company needed some tender loving care and that has been given in recent years.

Compared to Johnnie Walker, the Dewar house style tends to be a softer blend with the sweeter heather honey notes of Aberfeldy single malt at its heart. This is very approachable, easy to drink whisky that can take ice and a mixer, while also being enjoyable on its own or with a little water.

Dewar's make great play of 'marrying' their whiskies prior to final bottling – a process developed by their first Master Blender A. J. Cameron back in the early twentieth century. Today it involves making up the blend and placing it for up to six months in special marrying casks so that the flavours are fully and harmoniously integrated. The company insist that while their instruments can't detect any difference in flavour their human tasting panel can and so they stick with this time-consuming and expensive extra stage. They're not the only people doing this, but it is unusual and appears to make a real difference.

You can learn more about all of this on their website or by visiting their very smart visitor centre at the Aberfeldy distillery. I can admit here that I was involved in its creation (and very proud of it I am, too) but that was quite some while ago, so I feel completely free to praise this whisky wholeheartedly and without any embarrassment.

Colour A rich golden whisky, and stylish packaging.

Nose Full and fruity; raisins, orange peel, toffee/butter fudge and heathery hints.

Taste A rich, fruity sweetness; good length and weight; hints of oak, citrus notes, honey and caramel.

Finish Full flavoured, long and lingering, with liquorice notes.

Verdict

35

Producer
Distillery
Visitor Centre

Availability

Price

John Dewar & Sons Ltd
n/a – this is a blend
Dewar's World of Whisky,
Aberfeldy, Perthshire
Good in the USA, duty free
and specialists in the UK
◻◻◻◼◼

www.dewars.com

Dewar's
Signature

I have deliberately not recommended many expensive whiskies here, believing that there is plenty to explore below £100 a bottle and that, once you get well into three figures, a disproportionate amount of the cost goes into lavish packaging (on which everyone in the distribution chain takes a margin). Moreover, there is a danger that you can pay a significant premium simply for rarity or age, without necessarily seeing a commensurate improvement in the whisky.

Signature (it's the original John Dewar's, by the way, though I fancy his flamboyant son Tommy would have liked the style of this) does have rather a lavish wooden box and fancy stopper, and it will typically cost you around £200 in the UK (try and find it at the airport instead). But, for those special occasions and if you like this style of whisky, it's worth it.

Like Johnnie Walker Blue Label (its closest competitor) this is non-aged: that is to say that while the blend has some very old whiskies, mainly Aberfeldy, it also has some younger ones and the blenders think you probably wouldn't pay the price if they put the age on the bottle. And even if they don't think that, the marketing people certainly do.

Once again, the whiskies in Signature are married (see Dewar's 12 Years Old for an explanation) and this, together with the high percentage of single malt, accounts for the smooth, rich taste. It's one to sip and savour after a celebration dinner.

Keep the posh wooden box, by the way; it makes a handy coffin for a pet hamster or gerbil.

Colour Deep golden amber.

Nose Sweet, balanced, rich and fruity, fudge, coffee crème brûlée and vanilla ice cream drizzled with warm toffee sauce. The aromas develop with nougat, toasted macadamia nut, marzipan and lashings of honey.

Taste Rich, sweet and long with a velvety, creamy mouth feel. Butter toffee and honey with warm winter fruits and mellow tones of sultanas, raisins, apples and coconut. Full bodied and velvety.

Finish A long and complex finish. Smooth and warming.

Verdict

36

Producer	The Sazerac Company
Distillery	Buffalo Trace, Franklin County, Kentucky
Visitor Centre	Yes
Availability	Specialists
Price	☐☐☐■☐

www.buffalotrace.com see also www.bourbonwhiskey.com

Eagle Rare
17 Years Old

American whiskey brands can be confusing to the outsider: first seen in 1975, Eagle Rare was originally a 101-proof 10-year-old Kentucky straight bourbon whiskey (not single-barrel) from Seagram and thus among the last new bourbon brands introduced prior to the current era of so-called 'small batch' releases. Subsequently, Eagle Rare has been distilled, bottled and/or marketed by a number of companies, including the Old Prentice Distillery of Frankfort, Kentucky.

The Sazerac Company, a New Orleans-based producer and importer and the parent company of five distilleries, acquired Eagle Rare from Seagram in March 1989. At that time, Sazerac's Kentucky distillery was known as the George T. Stagg Distillery but today carries the name Buffalo Trace (see separate entry).

There are two versions: a 10 Years Old and this older, more expensive big brother, part of Buffalo Trace's Antique Collection. It will come as no surprise to whisky enthusiasts that this book keeps referring back to Buffalo Trace as the source for some outstanding whiskies but it is perhaps not as well known (yet) to the general consumer as it should be, and the plethora of brand names and identities don't help.

Be that as it may, 17-year-old bourbon is a rare and precious thing. Most bourbon matures much faster than this, due to the Kentucky climate, so age alone attracts a fairly stiff premium, though, in fairness to the distiller, it must be remembered that evaporation losses are higher here than in Scotland. At 17 years this is probably reaching its peak and, for sheer smoothness, has few equals.

Inevitably there is variation from batch to batch, as this is produced in small quantities, but the overall standard is exceptionally high and lovers of great, full-flavoured bourbon looking for well-balanced maturity are unlikely to feel disappointed.

Colour Deep, rich, copper gold.
Nose Honey, caramel and marzipan.
Taste Lots of weight and body; sweetness then orange and vanilla fudge.
Finish Extended finish, surprisingly drying to the end.

Verdict

37

Producer	Heaven Hill
Distillery	Bernheim, Louisville, Kentucky
Visitor Centre	Yes
Availability	Specialists
Price	☐■☐☐☐

www.heaven-hill.com see also www.bardstownwhiskeysociety.com

Elijah Craig
12 Years Old

At 12 years old and 94 proof, Elijah Craig is bottled exclusively from a dumping of 70 barrels or less, all drawn from the middle to upper floors of Heaven Hill's traditional metal-clad rick houses. The distillery proudly claims that this is the original small batch bourbon, having been created before the term was invented. Elijah Craig was recently awarded Double Gold at the San Francisco World Spirits Competition and has been a winner in *Whisky Magazine*'s Best of the Best tasting competition.

There's an interesting story behind the name. The Reverend Elijah Craig was born in Orange County, Virginia, sometime around 1740 (accounts vary, as if you cared). He was ordained a Baptist preacher in 1771 and must have been a lively character because he was apparently imprisoned briefly in South Carolina after being charged with disturbing the peace during his sermons!

Later he led a congregation to Scott County, Kentucky, and planned the settlement that would eventually be known as Georgetown. Quite the proto-typical social entrepreneur, old Elijah founded a number of businesses including a small distillery that converted bulky grain into whiskey – higher value and easier to transport and trade. Among his ventures was the Royal Spring Mill and, so the story goes, a fire there led to barrels being charred. Rather than discard them, the parsimonious cleric employed them to age his whiskey. (Quite why the barrels burnt from the inside is a mystery: we'll attribute it to divine intervention.)

Anyway, in honour of his contribution to whiskey, Craig is considered a 'Father of Bourbon' and Heaven Hill named this premium expression after him. That's all. It's a pretty fair memorial, however, since it's rightly very highly rated and a great-value bottle.

Colour A rich, warming golden brown.
Nose Lots going on here, with caramel and honey to the fore. Sweet but not cloyingly so.
Taste Agreeably complex, lots of oak notes, spiced fruits and jam. Very smooth and mouth coating.
Finish Vanilla sweetness; lingering pleasantly and holding together well. Yummy!

Verdict

38

Producer	Glenora Distillery
Distillery	Glenora Inn & Distillery, Glenville, Cape Breton, Nova Scotia, Canada
Visitor Centre	Yes
Availability	Specialists
Price	◼◼◼◻◻

www.glenoradistillery.com

Glen Breton

Rare

Oops! Our very first 'glen' and it's not from Scotland.

But, be honest, do you think a bottle reading 'Canada's Only Single Malt Whisky' and bearing a large red maple leaf on the front, together with the words 'Canadian/Canadien' could be mistaken for Scotch? Would you pick up a bottle, get it home and then think 'D'oh'? The Scotch Whisky Association (SWA) certainly thought so and fought a long and expensive court battle to have the word 'glen' removed from this product, thus protecting you from the consequences of your own foolishness.

A little harsh, you may feel, since this comes from Glenville in Nova Scotia and the distillery's president is one Lauchie MacLean – there's little doubt who settled this part of Canada, and it wasn't the French. And Glen Ora can only make 250,000 litres of spirit annually and, for their Glen Breton, they use copper pot stills and barley, yeast and water to make their single malt whisky which is notably different from most Canadian whisky.

Eventually the case was lost, though it did go all the way to the Canadian Supreme Court and the SWA seemed to me less than magnanimous in defeat. Anyway, now you can buy Canadian Single Malt Whisky in Scotland. Few off-licences reported queues of excited would-be Mounties and lumberjacks, however, and the Scotch whisky industry seems to have survived this less than convulsive shock.

According to Glen Ora spokesman Bob Scott, the company will now 'demonstrate the special ability of the Gaelic Scots of Cape Breton to craft an exceptional single malt whisky, which is uniquely Canadian'.

We await this David-and-Goliath-type struggle with interest.

Colour Golden Amber.
Nose Butterscotch, heather, honey and ground ginger.
Taste Creamy with a good flow of toasty wood, almond and caramel.
Finish Rounded, lingering, faintly sweet, the merest whisper of peat.

Verdict

39

Producer	G & J Grant
Distillery	Glenfarclas, Ballindalloch, Banffshire
Visitor Centre	Yes
Availability	Specialists
Price	■■■□□

www.glenfarclas.co.uk

Glenfarclas

21 Years Old

Scottish readers may now relax – this 'glen' is frae Bonnie
Scotland, as in the glens of home. No relation to the Grants
of Glenfiddich fame but, like their namesakes, the Grants of
Glenfarclas are an example of a dying breed: the independent,
family-owned distiller.

Not that there seems any danger of that changing in the near
future, as the next generation of the family is already in the
business and will presumably inherit the reins in due course.
Current Chairman John L. S. Grant is the fifth member of the
family to own and manage the distillery, and his son George S.
Grant is working as the company's Brand Ambassador (great
job, by the way – you travel round the world drinking whisky
with people, though presumably there's more to it than that).

The key point about this family ownership is continuity, both in
distilling style and in management. With freedom from short-
term shareholder pressure, companies like this (and the
Glenfiddich Grants) can build stocks and take a long-term view
of their business.

With Glenfarclas this has paid off with the release of their
Family Casks series – individual cask bottlings representing
every year continuously from 1952 to the present day. Some
of the older whiskies are excellent and excellent value, even if
they breach my self-imposed £1,000 per bottle mark. But I'm
not going to recommend one of those, tempted though I am to
do so. As an introduction to the Glenfarclas style of sherry-aged
Speyside whisky, try the sublime 21 Years Old. At less than £60
it's a steal, though I'd personally like to see it offered at a higher
strength than 43% abv. That's nit-picking, though: if you like
full-flavoured, rich but not aggressive whiskies that just ooze
class (and why wouldn't you?) this one is definitely for you.

Colour Noticeably dark; the sherry casks have been
at work here.

Nose Sherry nose, fruit cake, oranges and sweetness.
Not a hint of over-age or rubber.

Taste Very full and rounded; old leather, dried fruits
and dark marmalade. Layered.

Finish A rich, rolling finish.

Verdict

40

Producer	G & J Grant
Distillery	Glenfarclas, Ballindalloch, Banffshire
Visitor Centre	Yes
Availability	Specialists
Price	⬜⬛⬜⬜⬜

www.glenfarclas.co.uk

Glenfarclas

105

I haven't listed too many cask strength whiskies, because they're often quite hard to find, but this is clearly one to try and represents great value for money, too. The appeal of the 'cask strength' bottle is that you are able to try whisky just as you would if you sneaked into the warehouse and got a dram straight from the barrel. It hasn't been filtered, which inevitably removes some of the natural body from the whisky, and self-evidently it hasn't been diluted.

Strictly speaking, Glenfarclas 105 isn't cask strength because it is bottled at 60% abv, but that is near enough and, as this isn't a single-cask bottling, they standardise the strength for consistency. It's probably one of the easiest of the very high-strength whiskies to find and was one of the very first to offer this style, so it gets marks just for that.

So this is strong stuff. But the point is not to indulge in macho posturing and drink it at this strength (though you've got to try a wee sip). Rather you should dilute it to your taste and still pick up all the oily richness that is whisky's natural condition. And, while you're doing it, help support that rarest of beasts: an independent, family-owned, Scottish Scotch whisky company. Hurrah!

Glenfarclas are great advocates of sherry casks and this is a minor classic from a family company justifiably proud of their independence. They jealously, and rightly, guard their reputation for quality and you won't ever see anything second-rate with their label.

The distillery is well worth a morning of your time if you're ever in the area.

Colour Deep gold revealing maturation in top quality ex-sherry casks.

Nose Clearly a big whisky, fruity with wine notes, caramel and chocolate.

Taste Sherry wood clearly but honey in the background; sweet chocolate and dried fruits.

Finish Some smoky hints, lingering wine notes and honey shows through.

Verdict

41

Producer	William Grant & Sons Distillers Ltd
Distillery	Glenfiddich, Dufftown, Banffshire
Visitor Centre	Yes
Availability	Worldwide
Price	▪▪▪☐☐

www.glenfiddich.com

Glenfiddich
18 Years Old

Glenfiddich is the best-selling single malt whisky in the world, thanks to a far-sighted decision by this staunchly independent, family-owned company to start promoting single malt whisky well before the industry giants. It's generally said that serious efforts to sell Glenfiddich started in the 1960s but I have seen a promotional bottle pourer from before World War 2, suggesting that at least some lucky drinkers were converted to the appeal of this splendid dram in an age of ubiquitous blends.

Be that as it may, Glenfiddich's all-pervading presence actually serves to put off some malt fans, who argue that something so popular can't really be that good. Because Glenfiddich is seen everywhere (and it really is) it loses its snob appeal.

But any whisky anorak taking this approach is missing some rare treats. As a family-owned company, William Grant & Sons have been able to take a long-term approach to the stewardship of their whisky, without the pressure of half-year earnings reports to a greedy and often short-sighted City. The result is that the company have extensive stocks of older Glenfiddichs, which are arguably under-appreciated by some drinkers and thus represent something of a bargain.

If your wallet will stretch, the 30 Years Old variant is simply outstanding (in fact, read on). But, for affordable everyday drinking that gives real pleasure, look no further than this 18 Years Old. It's Speyside at its best; a great example of a classic whisky from a distiller to whom all whisky fans the world over owe a sincere and extended vote of thanks.

Colour Rich, warm gold.
Nose A classic Speyside – fruity, fragrant and with a very clean nose.
Taste Lots to find here: apples, sharp citrus notes but plenty of depth also, with dark fruit and oak.
Finish Elegant and well defined.

Verdict

42

Producer	William Grant & Sons Distillers Ltd
Distillery	Glenfiddich, Dufftown, Banffshire
Visitor Centre	Yes
Availability	Worldwide
Price	☐☐☐☐■

www.glenfiddich.com

Glenfiddich
30 Years Old

I know, another Glenfiddich. How boring.

Wrong! Wrong! Wrong!

Forget your prejudices. At around £200 in most UK outlets (less in duty free) this is good value, if not quite the serious bargain it was just a few years ago. It doesn't come in a fancy box with a numbered bottle but this was a worthy and decisive overall winner of the 2007 Scottish Field Merchant's Challenge.

As we've learned, Glenfiddich is still a family-owned company and is staunchly independent. They have extensive stocks and a single-minded way of doing things. Many of their people have been with them for decades (some have even had several generations of the same family working for the company) and this means there is a rare continuity in thinking, custom and practice.

I don't want to suggest they're 'stick in the mud' or resistant to progress, but there is a sense in which their very immunity to fads and fashion makes them fashionable. Mind you, the distillery hosts an annual contemporary arts programme, which can lead to some unusual sights, such as fire buckets hanging halfway up the still house wall and a stack of cars held together by binding tape, so they're quite prepared to take some risks with their image. Anyway, back to the whisky.

This stuff oozes flavour. The late Michael Jackson, revered in whisky circles, described it as 'luxurious, but in a restrained, understated way', which sort of describes the company as well. Glenfiddich do 40 and 50 Years Old versions as well: they are a great deal more expensive and, for bang for your buck, you'd do well to stop right here.

Colour Dark and enticing.
Nose Beguilingly fresh and fruity; spicy with sherry notes.
Taste Medium body but mouth coating; tropical fruit, honey, spice and fresh fruits, followed by some darker notes
Finish All of the above; hints of oak and a touch of smoke in there for good measure.

Verdict

43

Producer
Distillery

Visitor Centre

Availability
Price

Glenglassaugh Distillery Co. Ltd
Glenglassaugh, Portsoy,
Aberdeenshire
None at time of writing,
but plans are in hand.
Tours available
Specialists
□■□□□

www.glenglassaugh.com

Glenglassaugh
The Spirit Drink That Dare Not Speak Its Name

Glenglassaugh was mothballed in 1986 but, to general surprise, reopened at the end of 2008 under new ownership and after a healthy investment to get the old place going.

And now, here's a confession. Well, two actually.

I worked on the planning and development of this product so if you feel that disbars me from comment stop reading now. And it's not actually whisky, so again you might want to look away.

This is what used to be known in distilleries as 'clearic' – new make spirit straight off the still. It will become whisky but it can't be called whisky until it has spent a minimum of three years (and not a day less) in oak barrels in a warehouse in Scotland. Up until 1915, when the ageing regulations became law, a lot of 'whisky' would have been drunk like this and, until the advent of more responsible health and safety at work practices in the 1970s, a lot was drunk in distilleries in the infamous practice of 'dramming'. Quite a lot probably still is, if you know where to look, who to ask and can keep your mouth shut. (Not while you're drinking, obviously.)

So, if you want to know how whisky starts life, you have to try this. One or two distilleries sell their new make but, in my opinion (and not just because I was involved), this is the best. It's fruity, very clean and aromatic, and surprisingly complex, so should age well. Bottled at 50% abv it's not at all harsh or spirity and dilutes nicely. There is also a version bottled after 6 months ageing in red wine casks that has a pleasant rosé blush colour.

As you try it you can ponder the thought that this is what great-grandad probably drank.

Colour Colourless, slight clouding on addition of water. Look for well-defined viscimetric whorls.

Nose Creamy butterscotch and custard creams give way to delicate notes of sweet hay and freshly cut grass. With water, this spirit becomes very floral and fruity.

Taste Powerful at first with a wave of chilli and black pepper, then toffee and liquorice.

Finish Fresh and fruity on the nose; spicy yet sweet on the palate.

Verdict

44

Producer
Distillery

Visitor Centre

Availability
Price

Glenglassaugh Distillery Co. Ltd
Glenglassaugh, Portsoy,
Aberdeenshire
None at time of writing, but
plans are in hand. Tours available
Specialists
▪▪▪▪▫

www.glenglassaugh.com

Glenglassaugh
26 Years Old

Yes, I know I've mentioned this tiny distillery already and I know this whisky is both expensive and hard to find – but it's worth it. This is one of my personal all-time favourites and, while I would probably never have discovered it if I hadn't done some work for the distillery (this is the disclaimer clause) this doesn't disqualify me.

What you will experience here is the subtle and charming effect of long ageing in good wood on a fragrant and delicate new spirit. Back when this was distilled, sometime prior to 1986, virtually all of Glenglassaugh's output was going for blending, mainly in Cutty Sark. This isn't a strongly flavoured or particularly highly coloured whisky, so the blenders weren't looking for pronounced flavour from the blend components, more nuances and some complexity.

So they tended to use 'refill' casks; that is to say, barrels that might once have held either sherry or bourbon but had been used at least once (and possibly more often) for Scotch whisky. Then, as happens from time to time, not all the Glenglassaugh was used and a quantity was left quietly ageing.

In this particular case, and this doesn't always happen, it just got better and better with age. So, when the new owners took over, they bottled the remaining casks and released, first a 21 Years Old and then this 26 Years Old version. When it's gone it will be gone and the world will be a poorer place. Either is worth tracking down.

In fact, grab some now while you still can. It's a creamy, complex, slightly sweet whisky that I find quite bewitching, especially as a late-night reward after a particularly trying day. The distillery character is clearly evident, but some more sherry casks have got into this batch, adding richness and depth.

Colour Warm straw. Darker than the 21 Years Old.

Nose Very delicate; dried fruits and noses younger than the age would suggest.

Taste Complex and multi-layered, spice notes dancing with rich fruits and caramel; superb balance.

Finish Vanilla notes carry the freshness through into a long and slightly spicy finish that is influenced but never dominated by the sherry casks.

Verdict

45

Producer	Ian Macleod Distillers Ltd
Distillery	Glengoyne, Dumgoyne,
	nr Kilearn, Glasgow
Visitor Centre	Yes
Availability	Specialists
Price	☐☐☐☐☐

www.glengoyne.com

Glengoyne
21 Years Old

I have a great fondness for Glengoyne for no better reason than it was the first distillery I ever visited. It was on my honeymoon, as it happened, which should have alarmed my wife, though whisky didn't start to play a big part in my life until some years later. She does mention it from time to time, however.

All this was rather more than 21 years ago, so we presumably got something right. The distillery itself has taken on a new lease of life since it was sold by the Edrington Group to the current owners, who have invested heavily in the excellent visitor facilities, increased production and new products.

They make much of the fact that all the malt they use is totally unpeated. Until recently, they also highlighted their use of Golden Promise barley, traditionally highly rated for making whisky, but low yielding and prone to disease. In fact, for many years The Macallan also emphasised a commitment to Golden Promise but, as production expanded, both they and Glengoyne have discreetly dropped it. So think of this as a farewell to this old-fashioned variety.

Non-peated malt, says the distillery, means you get 'the real taste of malt'.

Whatever the truth of that, this is a very attractive whisky that deserves to be better known. It's available at various ages but really comes into its own with this 21 Years Old style. If you really want to splash out there is also a 40 Years Old, in a rather nice decanter, but the price of that one isn't printable here. For the same money you can get nearly 50 bottles of this little beauty and I know what I would rather have.

Colour	Glorious old gold. The judicious use of 100% sherry oak gives richness and depth.
Nose	Sweet and honeyed; sherry, ripe apples and maybe baked apple pie.
Taste	Toffee, vanilla and rich sherry notes initially, giving way to some spice and a very pleasant warming glow. 'Stewed pears and custard' have been reported.
Finish	Quite extended, smooth and warming, with gentle spice hints as it fades.

Verdict

46

Producer	LVMH
Distillery	Glenmorangie, Tain, Ross-shire
Visitor Centre	Yes
Availability	Different expressions widely available
Price	■■□□□

www.glenmorangie.com

Glenmorangie
Quinta Ruban

Glenmorangie's long-term owners (mainly the MacDonald family) sold out to the French luxury marketing house Louis Vuitton Moet Hennessy (LVMH) in October 2004 for £300m, a price which excited some comment.

Previously, the company had something of a schizophrenic personality: trying to maintain Glenmorangie and, to a lesser extent Ardbeg, as premium whiskies but also attempting to compete with cheaper blends and fulfilling substantial supermarket business. However, LVMH are more single-mindedly a luxury brand operation; the difference between 'premium' and 'luxury' being a wide one culturally and in terms of both price and target consumer.

As a result, they have reduced effort on blends, sold the Glen Moray distillery and brand, and reformulated, repackaged and relaunched the Glenmorangie range in an attempt to seduce more international buyers looking for a luxury spirit.

According to research analysts IWSR, Glenmorangie steadily lost market share from 2000 to 2008, underperforming the global growth in single malt whisky retail sales value, and the slippage appears to have continued while the brand was being repositioned. That's hardly surprising, given the time these things take, but it remains to be seen if the new strategy will work – certainly malt fans were divided on the merits of the new look. However, the real decision will be taken by the elusive and dangerously fickle luxury consumers of the Far East and the volatile BRIC markets.

Of the whiskies, the Quinta Ruban is perhaps the most interesting. Glenmorangie pioneered the now wildly fashionable practice of finishing whiskies in alternative casks with their first Port Wood finish back in 1990. That was good; this is an improvement – if no longer the original, it's still the best.

Colour A rich, warm reddish gold.
Nose Archetypal Glenmorangie delicacy and complexity with a new depth.
Taste Great balance; complexity and richness; fruit notes, chocolate and an underlying, delicate sweetness.
Finish A lingering and enigmatic finish that intrigues; chocolate orange rush at the end.

Verdict

47

Producer	Gordon & MacPhail
Distillery	n/a
Visitor Centre	Retail Shop, South Street, Elgin, Morayshire
Availability	Specialists
Price	▢▢▢▢▢

www.gordonandmacphail.com

Gordon & MacPhail

Glen Grant 25 Years Old

The observant reader will, by now, have observed that all the entries in this book are for official proprietary bottlings and not those of so-called 'third party' merchants. There are several reasons for this, not least availability and the greater danger of variability in independent bottlings. But I must make one exception, for the world's greatest merchant bottler: Gordon & MacPhail of Elgin.

James Gordon and John Alexander MacPhail announced the opening of their 'centrical and commodious premises' on South Street, Elgin in May 1895, promising their customers 'the utmost satisfaction' and guaranteeing 'a superior article at a popular price'. Here's the thing: it's still true. Buy anything with their label on it and you'll be happy. Promise.

Today, as they have done for more than a hundred years, G&M buy fillings – that is to say, they provide or specify the casks into which is racked 'new make' bought direct from the distillers. It is then stored either by the distiller concerned or in G&M's own extensive warehouses and bottled as and when G&M consider it to be ready. Because this has been their policy since the earliest years, they have extensive stocks of rare and very old whisky. In fact they claim to carry possibly the largest range of whiskies in the world, a comprehensive selection of which may be seen at the Elgin shop. This is a veritable cathedral of whisky: grown men have been known to break down in tears here and have to be removed gently to a place of safety.

Sadly, I can only pick one of their whiskies, so I'm going for their bottling of a 25 Years Old Glen Grant. It's cracking value and demonstrates how great this distillery can be when the whisky is properly aged. It seems churlish to pick fault with this, but if they'd only bottled it at 46%, this would be outstanding. Don't let that stop you, though.

Colour Warm and rich.

Nose Dark fruits, cake and chocolate.

Taste Full-bodied but never overwhelming, this is complex, rich and slightly sweet.

Finish Very consistent; a long, rolling finish with citrus hints and jammy red fruit.

Verdict

48

Producer

Distillery
Visitor Centre

Availability
Price

Irish Distillers Group for
Mitchell & Son
Midleton, Cork, Ireland
Retail shop at the CHQ Building,
Dublin
Rare
■■■□□

www.mitchellson.com

Green Spot

This is a legendary Irish whiskey, spoken of in hushed and reverent tones. Despite the fact that it is hard to find (only 6,000 bottles are made each year), I have to recommend this. Though I'm breaking one of my own rules, this is so special that an exception has to be made.

Think of the coelacanth. A living fossil that was supposed to have died out millions of years ago yet turned up in a fishing net and astounded scientists. Well, this is the coelacanth of whisky – a dogged survivor of a virtually extinct race of giants.

For this is Irish pot still whiskey and, by rights, it shouldn't exist. A 'pot still' whiskey is one made in Irish copper stills (generally larger than those found in Scotland) using malted and unmalted barley (unlike Scotch, which is purely malted barley). This gives Irish pot still whiskeys a smooth and oily character, with a purity caused by triple distillation.

Traditionally, Irish retailers sold their own label of whiskey from a local distiller. But as the Irish distilling industry died out and was rationalised one by one, these idiosyncratic one-offs were snuffed out. Eventually only Mitchell's of Dublin kept going (although, at one time they were able to offer Blue, Yellow and Red Spot, as well). Today Green Spot is made exclusively for Mitchell's and entirely from seven- and eight-year-old Midleton pot still whiskey, with 25% of the spirit having matured in sherry casks.

For a while it was the sole survivor of this style of whiskey but today it has been joined by expressions from Redbreast and Midleton. The bottle isn't much to look at, but then a coelacanth is pretty ugly. Get inside the bottle, though, and you'll quickly change your mind.

Colour Pale gold.
Nose Greengage jam; clean.
Taste Quite unique! Waxy, lively and full of honey and minty notes; very clean.
Finish Disappears quite quickly, but the sweetness lingers with, curiously, some smoke.

Verdict

49

Producer	Suntory
Distillery	Hakushu, Japan
Visitor Centre	Yes
Availability	Specialists
Price	

THE
HAKUSHU
SINGLE MALT
WHISKY

AGED **18** YEARS

Distilled and matured in
Hakushu distillery surrounded by forest

PRODUCT OF JAPAN
SUNTORY LIMITED
ウイスキー

白州

"はくしゅう"

www.suntory.com

Hakushu
18 Years Old

Suntory's second distillery was built in 1973 in Hakushu at the foot of Mt Kaikomagatake in the Southern Japan Alps, surrounded by pine forests and close to fast-flowing mountain streams (hakushu means 'white sand banks' and white is Japan's most sacred colour). Hakushu Higashi (West) was added in 1981 and the single malt produced here is held in high regard, though the original plant was mothballed in 2006. For a brief period, this was said to be the largest single malt distillery in the world.

Twelve pot stills operate at Hakushu West and, in the Japanese manner, their varied design allows the distillery to produce spirit with a remarkably wide variety of flavours. Malt is prepared off site at Yamazaki, from grain brought from Scotland, but there are extensive visitor facilities at Hakushu with an interpretation centre, gift shop, restaurant and a museum, housed in a dramatic former malting noted for its distinctive and unusual double pagoda roof with linking bridge.

We see both the 12- and 18-year-old expressions in the UK with, very occasionally, sightings of the 25 Years Old and some limited bottlings in specialists. Any of these would be a fine introduction to Japanese whisky but try to find the 18-year-old version if possible, because the additional maturation has really added some extra dimensions to this fine whisky.

It has picked up significant awards from the International Wine & Spirits Competition (IWSC) and International Spirits Challenge and is very highly rated by most commentators. The style is quite delicate, attributed by some commentators to the impact on both distillation and maturation of the distillery's height above sea level (700 metres). Being neither a physicist nor a meteorologist I don't feel competent to comment on the accuracy of this intriguing observation.

Colour Pale gold.
Nose Sharp green apples; delicate and refined.
Taste Deceptively light bodied but with fruit and cereal in great balance. Peat merges with oak.
Finish Spicy and lingering. Some tasters remark on a resemblance to Irish pot still make.

Verdict

50

Producer	The Sazerac Company
Distillery	Buffalo Trace, Franklin County, Kentucky
Visitor Centre	Yes
Availability	Specialists
Price	▪▪▪▪▫

www.buffalotrace.com see also **www.kentuckybourbon.com**

Thomas H Handy

Sazerac Rye

You're going to find this both tricky to get and expensive, but bear with me.

In the United States, 'rye whiskey' is, by law, made from a mash of at least 51% rye. (The other ingredients of the mash are usually corn and malted barley.) It is distilled to no more than 160 (U.S.) proof (i.e. 80% abv) and aged in charred, new oak barrels. The whiskey must be put into such barrels at not more than 125 (U.S.) proof and spirit that has been aged like this for at least two years may be further designated as 'straight', as in 'straight rye whiskey'. So far, so good.

But interest in rye whiskey declined after Prohibition and never really recovered. Until very recently, that is, when it acquired a sort of cult status, helped by praise from a few critics. As a result, prices of old rye whiskey are rising about as fast as stocks are going down and, consequently, it is hard to find. There is a Sazerac 18 Years Old, of legendary repute, but it sells out as soon as bottles are put on the shelf.

For a different, but still remarkable, experience, try to get hold of this version. It's a limited annual release of six-year-old stock, non-chill filtered and bottled at very high strength. Inevitably, the whiskey will vary slightly from year to year. By the time you read this the 2010 bottling should be available.

These are very forceful, charismatic and big, high-impact whiskies from Buffalo Trace, not just due to the high strength but to the huge range of intense flavours that may take some while to adapt to, especially if you are expecting bourbon.

It's hard to comment on the taste of this as the 2010 release isn't available but it is highly unlikely to be a disappointment and is very definitely a whiskey with which to amaze your friends. Add a good quantity of water and expect blast of different aromas and flavours with a long, long finish.

Colour Dark gold.
Nose Maple syrup and molasses; vanilla and dried fruit.
Taste Oily, mouth coating, hints of liquorice and then ripe fruit.
Finish Peppery; drying and oak hints.

Verdict

51

Producer | Compass Box Whisky Company
Distillery | n/a – this is a blending house
Visitor Centre | n/a
Availability | Mainly UK, USA and France – but check online

Price | ☐☐☐☐☐

www.compassboxwhisky.com

Hedonism

This is my second pick from Compass Box – self-proclaimed 'artisan whisky makers'. Well, they are certainly great at blending and shrewd urban marketers, so is it mean-spirited to suggest that they are not quite the horny-handed sons of toil that that description would imply? You decide.

Hedonism is one of their 'Limited Release' range, which means I'm sailing close to one of my own rules, but you shouldn't have too much trouble tracking it down in good specialist whisky shops, on the web or from Compass Box's own website. What's unusual about it is that it is 100% blended grain whisky and, more than that, it's around 20 years old and taken from first-fill ex-bourbon casks.

Each release is made up as a limited batch with whiskies selected from Cameron Bridge (see separate entry) and Cambus distilleries, but availability is very much determined by Compass Box's ability to find casks and the owner's willingness to share them. Depending on your point of view, grain whisky is either Scotland's dirty little secret or, in Compass Box's words, a 'little-known treasure'.

This proves just how good it can be. If you really like it, then there is an even harder to find and much more expensive 'reserve' version called Hedonism Maximus. This has similar character but the flavours are much deeper, even sweeter and much more intense given the 42- and 29-year-old whiskies.

As we have come to expect from this innovative company, the packaging is as elegant and stylish as the stuff in the bottle. Like all limited release whiskies expect some batch variation.

Colour Mid gold.
Nose Vanilla and coconut.
Taste Sweet, velvety smooth with diaphanous waves of liquorice, Callard & Bowser toffee (remember those?), hints of orange and loaded with ex-bourbon vanilla and marzipan flavours.
Finish The aromas of chocolate, spice and coconut linger satisfyingly and hold together well.

Verdict

52

Producer	Suntory
Distillery	n/a – this is a blend
Visitor Centre	There are centres at Suntory's Yamazaki and Hakushu distilleries
Availability	Rare
Price	▨▨▨▢▢

✓

17 Years Old
SUNTORY
WHISKY
HIBIKI
A harmonious blend of specially aged whiskies

www.suntory.com

Hibiki
17 Years Old

Before moving on to the 30-year-old version of this product (see next entry), which is expensive and very hard to find, you might like to try its younger brother, which is altogether more affordable. You might also remember it from its appearance in the excellent Oscar-winning 2003 movie *Lost in Translation* (a breakthrough role for Scarlett Johansson, as if you cared).

Many who try this for the first time will admit to being seduced by the packaging, which is fair enough, as it is both very attractive and sufficiently different to draw attention to itself without being outré or unduly outrageous. Which probably doesn't sound that big a deal until you consider how many whiskies there are on the shelves, without even beginning to count other distilled spirits, let alone wine – you get the picture?

So well done to Suntory's resourceful marketing department, but all they've really done is given this stand-out whisky a bottle to match. Hibiki means 'harmony', apparently, and the distillery themselves describe this as 'a master blend of carefully selected full-bodied malt and grain whiskies. This multi-award-winning blend creates a profound aroma with an elegant and mellow woody richness, accompanied by sweet, long-lasting citrus flavour.'

For once, the hype is fully justified. In Japan, apparently, Hibiki 17 commands a premium above similarly aged single malts and I can well believe that this is so. It is really a very complete whisky, exceptionally easy to drink while at the same time remaining complex and somewhat alluring – there is an elusive quality to the taste and finish that is hard to pin down. Try and serve it blind to your friends and they will likely be amazed at the quality and will be forced to rethink their prejudices and preconceptions about Japanese whisky. This is world-class stuff – so try to imagine how good the 30 Years Old is going to be!

Colour Pale gold.
Nose Citrus hints, vanilla, oak and floral. Light but not insubstantial.
Taste Quite complex and slow to evolve, with pine resin sweetness, vanilla and toffee. Some salty hints as it opens. Develops with water or ice.
Finish Appears to finish quite quickly, then reappears to delight and perplex.

Verdict

53

Producer
Distillery
Visitor Centre

Availability
Price

Suntory
n/a – this is a blend
There are centres at Suntory's
Yamazaki and Hakushu distilleries
Rare
■■■■■

www.suntory.com

Hibiki
30 Years Old

What's the best blended whisky in the world? It's a Scotch, naturally. Well, not in the opinion of the judges at the World Whiskies Awards in 2007 and 2008 who awarded that title to this premium whisky from Suntory. Mind you, it shouldn't have been a complete surprise: Hibiki 30 also collected the highest level of award at the International Spirits Competition in 2004 and then again in 2006, 2007 and 2008. In 2007 they also picked up a Best in Class. These awards are judged blind, by the way, with a number of experienced judges so it's worth noting whiskies that win regularly.

Japanese blends are rather different from those produced in Scotland. Apart from the fact that the whisky tastes different, the smaller Japanese industry does not exchange or trade whiskies from different distilleries in the way that is the norm in Scotland. So companies rely on their own resources.

Fortunately for Suntory, their Yamazaki distillery has an unusual variety of stills, twelve in all in six different shapes and sizes, producing a wide range of flavours. To this they add the produce of Hakushu, Hibiki's home distillery, where again there are a number of different stills. And then they increase their options even more by using many different types of cask to mature the spirit, including Japanese Mizunara oak. As a result the blender has a remarkably wide variety of whiskies to choose from – in fact, more than 30 different whiskies are blended to create Hibiki, using grain whisky from Suntory's Chita distillery.

As you would expect, this is an expensive product (expect to pay £500–600 a bottle) and it will take a little bit of effort to track it down but it is, officially, the best blended whisky in the world. What else do you really need to know?

Colour	Deep beaten copper.
Nose	Raisin, figs and dates with a hint of Brazil nut and sweet dark cocoa.
Taste	Dark sweetness and a pleasant lingering woodiness.
Finish	Long, dark and very rich.

Verdict

54

Producer	Highland Distillers
Distillery	Highland Park, Kirkwall, Orkney
Visitor Centre	Yes
Availability	Pretty widely available
Price	☐☐☐☐☐

www.highlandpark.co.uk

Highland Park
18 Years Old

This is the first of four whiskies by Highland Park listed in this book. Four. From one distillery? Have I gone mad?

I don't think so. You could make a case that this is the best whisky in the world. Certainly it's won more awards than I can be bothered to count and at least one authority (Paul Pacult) thinks that Highland Park make 'the best spirit in the world'.

What is more, when I asked my 'oracles' Highland Park was their runaway winner, gathering nearly twice the nominations of any other brand. Quite a few of the people who voted for it are competitors so that is a pretty impressive endorsement.

But lacking Paul's ebullience and confident certainty, I'll content myself with saying it's pretty damn fine. You're going to have to look far and wide to beat this stuff. There are several reasons why. The distillery somewhat pretentiously refer to these as their 'five keystones' so we descend dangerously close to marketing speak here, but bear with me. They talk about traditional floor malting, aromatic peat, cool maturation, sherry oak casks and careful cask rotation.

Thing is, it's not just marketing froth. I've looked back in history and they were doing most of this stuff as early as 1924 and probably well before that, it's just that they didn't bang on about it. So, with Highland Park you get a very traditional style of whisky from a privately owned Scottish company in a funky, modern bottle that keeps getting better the more time you spend with it (the whisky, not the bottle).

Read on for three more whiskies from Highland Park and prepare to be amazed. Oh, and try and get to the distillery at least once in your life.

Colour Medium bright gold.
Nose A sweet, 'come hither' nose; sherry and marzipan.
Taste Fruity, rich, sweet and agreeably complex.
Great depth.
Finish Smoky hints fade gently into the background.

Verdict

55

Producer	Highland Distillers
Distillery	Highland Park, Kirkwall, Orkney
Visitor Centre	Yes
Availability	Exclusive to duty free shops, so you'll have to fly to buy it (sorry)
Price	■■■□□

✓

www.highlandpark.co.uk

Highland Park
21 Years Old

I'm not supposed to have favourites but, as you've realised by now, Highland Park is definitely one. Orkney is a special and unique place, with a string of islands linked by causeways, ferries and planes; ancient monuments scattered everywhere; a thriving and creative craft community; incredible light; unexpected panoramas at every turn; abandoned gun emplacements; amazing wildlife and two incredible distilleries.

Not to slight the nearby Scapa Distillery in any way (it's pretty good) but Highland Park is world-class. And it doesn't get any better, at least not within the bounds of most budgets, than their signature 21 Years Old expression.

This was a worthy winner of the 2009 World Whiskies Award for the World's Best Single Malt Whisky. I sat on the panel and it deserved every mark it got. Highland Park is noted for incredible balance, long development and a subtle peat smoke that continues to engage and tantalise and reward your taste buds the more time you spend with it. It's not the forceful peat of Islay but a more complex and refined flavour that the obsessives at Highland Park maintain is only possible by burning three different types of peat from their own peat bog.

But watch out! After the success of this whisky, demand increased greatly and the bottling strength was reduced from 47.5% abv to a standard 40% so you may not be drinking the whisky that garnered all the praise. There's nothing wrong with the latest bottlings, but some old stock might be available – if you see it, snap it up.

STOP PRESS: The latest news from Orkney is that they'll shortly be reverting to the higher strength so check the small print on the label and get the really good stuff.

Colour	Natural colour; the distillers say 'reddish gold Orkney sunset' but that's a bit fanciful!
Nose	Butterscotch, dark chocolate and orange.
Taste	Lush, full flavour and great balance with candied orange peel and spicy dark chocolate, leading to a rich smoky sensation with hints of roasted nuts. A honeyed sweetness.
Finish	Rich, complex and sweet smoky sensation then soft, medium-dry finish.

Verdict

56

Producer	Highland Distillers
Distillery	Highland Park, Kirkwall, Orkney
Visitor Centre	Yes
Availability	Pretty widely available in specialist retailers
Price	▢▢▢■■

www.highlandpark.co.uk

Highland Park
30 Years Old

Here goes whisky number three from Highland Park and we are moving into the realms of the truly sublime – and, what is more, truly sublime value. Yes, a bottle of this will cost close to £200 but the equivalent in chateau bottled claret would be several times that and there's every bit as much tradition, craftsmanship and quality in this bottle. And, if you're looking for value, this bottle will last rather longer than the claret, especially as it comes at a healthy 48.1% abv.

Fortunately, the distillery has pretty good stocks of these older whiskies and this lets us taste a more traditional style of whisky making. For a while, Highland Park flirted with reduced peating levels, as most of the spirit was destined for blending lighter styles such as Cutty Sark, but that isn't the case here.

Age has tempered the distinctive Highland Park smoke but it's still clearly evident, just more subtle. And I like that. One personal difficulty that I have with some of the more aggressively peated styles is just that – aggressive peating, which for me can often be overly dominant, masking inherent spirit character. It's like a giant steamroller on the palate.

No danger of that here. There is some brooding smokiness, but it is balanced by sweetness and great vitality and freshness for a whisky of this age. The extra strength means it's attractively full in flavour and, unusually for an older whisky, can stand the careful addition of water to bring out the more aromatic notes. Some skilled distilling has been complemented by good wood selection and careful warehousing, and the result is a stellar whisky that is worth every penny.

Colour Dark.

Nose Warming and round; honey and smoke.

Taste Beautifully balanced and full bodied; honey, vanilla, oak and smoke dancing through the palate but never dominating.

Finish All of the above gracefully combine, fading out with spice and whiffs of gentle smoke.

Verdict

57

Producer	Highland Distillers
Distillery	Highland Park, Kirkwall, Orkney
Visitor Centre	Yes
Availability	Surprisingly easy to find in specialists, given the age and price!
	☐☐☐☐■
Price	

www.highlandpark.co.uk

Highland Park
40 Years Old

Take a seat: this is the most expensive whisky in this book. Expect to pay around £800 for a bottle. For that you get a handsome box, leather bound booklet and a 48.3% abv spirit that deservedly won the 2009 World Whiskies Award for World's Best New Release.

The rule here is that I won't recommend anything over £1,000 and anything in three figures needs careful thought. But you don't need to hesitate. Buy this with confidence – in my view (and this is shared by a good part of the whisky community) this is simply as good as it gets. With the change from the £1,000 you can buy some pretty fine drams but this 40 Years Old wants to be set aside for very special occasions and very special friends. Having said that, you'll make a special friend out of anyone you serve this to (provided they have any kind of critical judgement) and you should drink it – don't just set it on a shelf and gaze wonderingly upon it. Appreciate, don't venerate is the motto here.

This is an exceptionally complex and refined whisky with multiple layers of flavour that will open up in the mouth and on the finish as you carefully sip and savour your dram. And, the next time you go back to it, you'll find something more and something different. Highland Park 40 just keeps on growing and developing and rewards careful study.

But I don't want you to think of this as hard work. Above all, this is a whisky to enjoy. Not every day, of course, but it really is a whisky to try before you die. And then put that off, at least until you finish the bottle.

Colour Mid gold. Using refill casks, time has added colour very slowly.

Nose Surprisingly delicate and refined; still fresh and distinctively 'Highland Park' with honey, chocolate and soft smoke.

Taste If a whisky can possess 'the X factor' this has got it – just sensationally complex and alluring. Superb balance and wave after wave of flavour, with no one element dominant.

Finish After showing more heather honey sweetness and hints of citrus, the smoke floats back for a last hurrah.

Verdict

58

Producer	Whyte & Mackay Ltd
Distillery	Isle of Jura, Craighouse, Jura
Visitor Centre	Yes – and a luxurious
	(for which read 'expensive')
	holiday apartment
Availability	Specialists
Price	☐■☐☐☐

www.isleofjura.com

Isle of Jura
Superstition

At the risk of offending the good folks at Whyte & Mackay, I'd say that, in general, the Isle of Jura single malts are nothing to get too excited about. They're pleasant enough but pretty bland, which, since this distillery was built in the 1960s to create employment on this lonely but beautiful island and serve the blending industry with a Speyside-style spirit, is no real surprise.

In recent years, though, they have made some efforts to raise their profile and the standard 10 Years Old is pretty widely seen. Don't bother with that, though. What you want, if you want anything, is Superstition.

This is a mixture of heavily peated whisky in the Islay style (not originally what Jura was built to produce) and some older casks that add warmth and subtlety. Accordingly, it doesn't carry an age statement, but don't let that or the name put you off. It's pleasantly different from the whiskies on nearby Islay.

Jura itself is notable for being home to less than 200 people and around 5,000 red deer. They wander about everywhere – mainly, it seems to me, on the island's one main road where they can be something of a hazard. Jura was also George Orwell's refuge when he escaped from London to write 1984 and the site of the infamous K Foundation Burn a Million Quid art event. Yes, rock musicians turned artists Bill Drummond and Jimmy Cauty quietly travelled to Jura and burnt £1m in £50 notes. As you would. Obviously.

With their fondness for special editions, Isle of Jura really ought to commemorate this: a very smoky dram at £50 a bottle would seem appropriate!

Colour	Deep bronze.
Nose	Wood smoke, bacon and freshly cut peat. Phenolic notes start to dominate.
Taste	Spice, honey, pine and peat flavours mingle with nuts and grassy/floral notes.
Finish	Smoke fades in again at the end.

Verdict

59

Producer	Irish Distillers Group
Distillery	Midleton, Cork, Ireland
Visitor Centre	Two! One in Dublin and one at Midleton Distillery, Cork
Availability	Specialists
Price	▪▪▪▪▫

www.jamesonwhiskey.com

Jameson
18 Years Old Limited Reserve

Jameson's is the best-selling brand of Irish whiskey and, under the ownership of corporate giants Pernod Ricard, has been expanding rapidly. The whiskies comprise a blend of pot still and grain spirit, all produced at the huge Midleton Distillery near Cork. With a bewildering range of stills, the plant is capable of producing a considerable variety of different styles, making the role of the Master Blender particularly significant, especially when a number of different casks come into play.

Though it's hardly cheap – a bottle of the 18 Year Old will set you back £70 – I just have to let this one through. I had the great privilege of tasting a release of this with Irish Distillers' Barry Crockett, who was brought up in a cottage in the distillery's grounds and today is Master Distiller at Midleton. That was well over a year ago but I believe I can still recall the taste, so distinctive a product is it.

The fact that it immediately picked up a clutch of significant awards proves that this was no flash in the pan. A combination of ex-bourbon and sherry barrels are used, and then they are aged according to the label for 'at least' 18 years. I can believe it: this is splendidly mature, without in any way exhibiting any signs of being overly woody or tired.

This is one of a larger range – there is a Special Reserve (12 years old), a Gold Reserve (non-aged but 13–14 years old on average), Signature Reserve (for duty free only), this Limited Reserve and finally, if your purse can stretch even further, a brilliant but confusingly named Rarest Vintage Reserve, which doesn't actually carry either an age or a vintage date, though it does (not very helpfully) carry the bottling date, currently 2007. You've got to love Irish marketing!

Colour Deep bronze.
Nose Aromatic Christmas cake, honey, vanilla and toffee.
Taste Cloves, nuts and nutty fudge, a wonderful balance; and the bourbon and oloroso sherry casks are beautifully integrated into a smooth and harmonious whole. Medium body but complex.
Finish Holds together well, as all the flavours linger nicely.

Verdict

60

Producer	Diageo
Distillery	n/a – this is a blend, but 'brand home' is Cardhu
Visitor Centre	Cardhu Distillery, Speyside (it's just along the road from The Macallan)
Availability	Everywhere – if you can't find this you're not trying very hard
Price	□■□□□

www.johnniewalker.com

Johnnie Walker
Black Label

In truth, this isn't one of my personal favourites. I find this Johnnie Walker expression and its little brother Red Label a little too harsh and smoky for my taste.

But you can't argue with success and this is one of the best-selling premium blends in the world. More to the point, if you ask around the whisky industry Black Label keeps coming up as a favourite or a whisky which other distillers and blenders admire. So, if you like big flavours then this is on your list.

Today Johnnie Walker is part of Diageo who, in 2009, controversially shut the door on close to 200 years of whisky history when they closed their Kilmarnock bottling plant, the traditional Walker home. Cue outrage from the locals and Scottish politicians but it doesn't appear to have made the slightest bit of difference to the worldwide legion of fans who probably neither know nor care where Kilmarnock is. Sorry, Kilmarnock.

The Black Label blend can be traced back to 1867 when Alexander Walker launched his 'Old Highland Whisky' in a distinctive square bottle and slanting black and gold label. The square bottle proved a great boon to the brand in developing export sales – because of the shape more bottles could be squeezed into any given space and shipping costs reduced. Of such simple things are legends made.

But there is a lot more to this than just clever packaging. Black Label succeeds not simply as a symbol of affluence and status in many markets but because for many it's the benchmark for a premium blend. This is a traditional whisky that's not to be under-estimated. Personally, I wouldn't take it to my desert island, but a lot of expert judges would.

Colour A medium bright gold.
Nose Maple sweetness with hints of smoke.
Malt and citrus.
Taste Robust and forceful, the peaty smoke to the fore but also dried fruits, sherry and vanilla; never unbalanced – power with discretion.
Finish Mellow, spicy and a great late-night dram.

Verdict

61

Producer	Diageo
Distillery	n/a – this is a blend, but 'brand home' is Cardhu Cardhu Distillery, Speyside
Visitor Centre	(it's just along the road from The Macallan)
Availability	Global, especially high-end, tax-free outlets
Price	◻◻◻◻■

www.johnniewalker.com

Johnnie Walker
Blue Label King George V Edition

Sometimes only luxury will do. Unadulterated, in-your-face, loadsamoney, show-off luxury.

Imagine you've got a Russian oligarch to impress, or a key business contact in the Far East needs a gift – that is the King George V Edition moment. Because this feels to me like an unashamedly flamboyant whisky for the nouveau riche. From the elaborate presentation packaging with the twin monogrammed studs you need to remove to open the huge box, to the deliberately theatrical ritual of opening its hidden double doors, the silk-lined interior with the parchment certificate, the crystal decanter on its matching plinth, and the meticulously detailed and very, very heavy cork stopper, it's all about the glamorous packaging.

Except, d'oh, this is also very good whisky. Did you imagine that the best-selling Scotch whisky in the world was going to put its name on any old gut rot, just because the box looks good (spectacular, to be honest)?

You can pay up to £1,000 for a single glass (yes, glass) of some Johnnie Walker styles but I maintain that's just showing off – flagship projects designed mainly for PR impact. So, for most of us, this must remain the ultimate Johnnie Walker. And very fine it is, too, as well it might be at approaching £400 a bottle.

So treat yourself at least once in your life and, as you sip, ask yourself, 'What are the poor people doing tonight?'

Colour   Deep and dark, suggestive of great age and some sherry casks in the blend.

Nose   Initially sweet, then more than a hint of smoke and lots of body. This is going to be BIG!

Taste   A very big, forceful whisky, surprisingly honeyed and well mannered, with the smoky Port Ellen coming through late. Still vibrant and complex, despite the age of some of the blend constituents.

Finish   A languorous, unhurried finish; very rounded, with the sweeter Speysiders complementing the last fading notes of peat smoke.

Verdict

62

Producer   Kilchoman Distillery Co. Ltd
Distillery   Kilchoman, Islay
Visitor Centre   Yes
Availability   Specialists and online
Price   ☐☐☐☐☐

www.kilchomandistillery.com

Kilchoman

I'm probably stretching my own rules here, because you're going to have to look really hard to find this, but the philosophy behind this book is to encourage entrepreneurs and innovators and to persuade you to look a little bit further for unusual and deserving spirits, so bear with me.

If we rule out the illicit manufacture of moonshine, this is probably as close as you can get to 'traditional' distilling, at least from the point of view of scale. Kilchoman is the first farmhouse distillery to be built in Scotland for a very long while, and the first on Islay for 124 years. There are now several similar projects in several different countries in various stages of completion, but Kilchoman was something of a pioneer and deserves respect and support for this, if nothing else.

The vision of enthusiast Anthony Wills, Kilchoman began distilling in 2005 and released its first whisky in 2009 (it sold new make spirit prior to that). All the barley used is grown on the neighbouring farm; there is a floor malting; none of the barrels leave the island during maturation; and the matured spirit is bottled on Islay. However, they can only make around 90,000 litres of spirit each year and so supplies are restricted: in fact, the Inaugural Release of just 8,300 bottles sold out within days. The already high prices promptly doubled on the secondary market as collectors vied for a bottle.

However, the initial wave of enthusiasm having passed, bottles of subsequent releases should be more accessible, if not widely found, but certainly not any cheaper. Try to track one down, impress your friends and support some real whisky people.

NB: The flavour of Kilchoman will develop over the various releases as the spirit matures, so the notes below are a guide, based on the Inaugural Release edition.

Colour Aged mainly in ex-bourbon barrels, so pale straw. Future releases may be darker.

Nose Surprisingly fruity, plenty of peat smoke but delicate citrus notes surprise.

Taste Creamy and mouth coating; dried fruits, smoke and toffee.

Finish Clean, refreshing, lingering smoke hints drift on for some time.

Verdict

63

Producer	Beam Global Spirits & Wine, Inc.
Distillery	Jim Beam, Clermont Distillery, Kentucky
Visitor Centre	Yes
Availability	Specialists and online
Price	▢▢▢▢■

www.knobcreek.com see also www.smallbatch.com

Knob Creek

Knob Creek is another small batch bourbon, distilled at the large Jim Beam distillery at Clermont, Kentucky. It gets its name, mildly titillating for UK drinkers in a vaguely smutty sort of a way, from a creek (stream) about 20 miles from the distillery that ran past Abraham Lincoln's boyhood home. Apparently, Lincoln's father worked in another nearby distillery and Lincoln himself was rescued from drowning in said stream. It seems that no one in the marketing department considered the alternative associations of the name outside of the USA.

Anyway, with that out of the way we can move on to the whiskey. This has achieved a sort of cult status, partly due to the astute management of recent shortages of stock creating additional pent-up demand. You can even buy a t-shirt, itself a limited edition, to commemorate the 'drought'.

Knob Creek was created by the legendary distiller Booker Noe in an attempt to create a pre-Prohibition style of bourbon and also, though the distillers tend to gloss over this bit, to come up with an American offering that would make bourbon fashionable again and compete with single malt Scotch.

In that, small batch bourbon has been a great success, with this 9-year-old, 50% abv product being one of the category leaders.

Others from Beam Global include Booker's, Basil Hayden's and Baker's. Naturally, their competitors have entered the market with their versions also. As the small batch handle suggests, supplies of these whiskies can be variable and there may be slight variations in style from batch to batch. It's all part of the charm and they're unlikely to be less than very good.

Colour Mid gold.
Nose Nutty, dark citrus and oak.
Taste Rich, full-bodied and complex. Some spice notes.
Finish A long, consistent finish with a lingering aftertaste.

Verdict

64

Producer	Diageo
Distillery	Lagavulin, Islay
Visitor Centre	Yes
Availability	Specialists and online
Price	■■■□□

www.malts.com

Lagavulin
16 Years Old

Aeneas MacDonald writes of a man who 'was kept awake for hours in the night by the prolonged rhapsodies of two Highlanders, men who had nothing else in common in the world but their affection for and praise of Lagavulin'. It has, he says, 'an almost legendary fame'. That was in 1930 and, if anything, its fame has grown. For fans of the richly phenolic, peaty, salty whiskies of Islay this is *primus inter pares*, though it must be allowed that Ardbeg runs close in the passion of its devotees.

Using barley malted at the nearby Port Ellen maltings (also Diageo), Lagavulin is distilled unusually slowly – a process that the makers claim gives 'the characteristic roundness and soft mellow edges' to the spirit. They certainly take their time over maturation, with the standard Classic Malts bottling being released at 16 years old. Rumour has it that Johnny Depp, the teetotal actor, will happily order a glass just to nose it, so striking is Lagavulin's aroma (it's not clear who gets to polish it off later). Michael Jackson famously described the nose as 'Lapsang Souchong and fruity sherry'. Sounds good, doesn't it?

Though there is a more expensive Distiller's Edition finished in Pedro Ximenez casks and a younger, high-strength version curiously, and unjustifiably, even more expensive still, this is the one you want. Marvel at its rich textures, prepare to be stunned by the waves of intense flavour and sit down before you take your first sip – this is potent stuff.

Read on for another stunning whisky from Lagavulin's next-door neighbour.

Colour Deep gold.
Nose Intense peat rush, followed by sweet oranges and toffee.
Taste A huge, mouth-filling whisky. Dry, then some sherried sweetness with toffee and a salty hint.
Finish Massive peat smoke and salty climax.

Verdict

65

Producer	Fortune Brands Inc.
Distillery	Laphroaig, Islay
Visitor Centre	Yes
Availability	Specialists and online
Price	☐■☐☐☐

www.laphroaig.com

Laphroaig
Quarter Cask

Laphroaig is the first of three distilleries you come to following the coast road round Islay out of Port Ellen and it presents a splendid sight. There is still a floor maltings on site and excellent visitor facilities (though you really want to eat in the Kiln Cafe at Ardbeg just along the road).

The Quarter Cask bottling is a splendid attempt to re-create a style of whisky that would have been more common a hundred or more years ago when smaller casks were used to mature spirit. This may have been because the firkin cask (holding nine gallons, or around 41 litres) was relatively freely available, due to its use in the brewing industry, or because the smaller cask was more popular for private sales or, as the distillery themselves like to suggest – rather romantically – because they were easier for smugglers to transport! Possibly, all three played their part.

The key point, however, is that whisky matures faster in a smaller cask and the wood has a greater influence (30% more according to the distillers). What is more, in their pursuit of tradition Laphroaig don't chill filter this whisky and they bottle it at a healthy 48% abv. Good on them.

It's a classic Islay malt – salty, peaty, phenolic and very full flavoured. Hugely impressive.

The result, in my opinion at least, is a huge improvement on the standard 10 Years Old (40% abv) – it's rounder, more vibrant, fuller and sweeter. Everything you look for in Laphroaig, in fact, and more, proving on this occasion, at least, that the old ways really were best.

Colour Quite pale, like beaten bronze.

Nose Tons of peat smoke, sweetness, coconut cream and some chocolate notes.

Taste Bold and assertive, full bodied and mouth coating (higher strength alcohol and non-chill filtering coming into play here) but gentle and sweet compared to the 10 Years Old.

Finish Amazingly extended finish, with the peat smoke and some coal fires coming into play. Spice notes and the distillery say 'zesty orange'. Beats me.

Verdict

66

Producer	J & A Mitchell & Co. Ltd
Distillery	Springbank, Campbeltown, Argyll and Bute
Visitor Centre	Yes
Availability	Specialists and online
Price	□■□□□

www.springbankwhisky.com

Longrow
CV

The original Longrow was an early casualty in Campbeltown's long and sorry decline, but the name at least was restored in 1973 when some heavily peated malt was distilled at Springbank to prove that Islay need not have a monopoly on this style. Eventually the idea caught on and Longrow is now distilled regularly, though not in great volume.

So you could say that Longrow is peated Springbank – except that it isn't. The fact that the malt is peated is clearly the key difference but, unlike Springbank, this undergoes a conventional double distillation. A mix of sherry and bourbon casks are used for maturation to contribute sweetness and spice before the peat takes over.

Longrow isn't exactly easy to find but the non-aged CV expression should turn up in specialists and it can be purchased online from the distillery's website. Like all of the company's 'standard' output, it's bottled at 46% abv and non-chill filtered – policies that I can only commend. The result is greater mouth feel in the whisky and a pleasing oiliness that speaks of the genuine article: would that more distillers would follow this lead. Note to consumers – it's worth the extra cost!

This is not the most subtle whisky you'll ever encounter but, despite its strength, many tasters find it goes well without adding water. If you like big, bold, assertive flavours and you've 'done' Islay then this is where you go next. If it appeals, there is a Longrow 100 Proof version, several aged expressions and the strange Gaja Barolo finish.

Colour Mid gold.
Nose Supreme balance between peat smoke, vanilla and cardamom.
Taste Bold and assertive; robust. Vanilla comes to the fore, then citrus (lemon marmalade?) and waves of spice and smoke.
Finish Surprisingly gentle and balanced, with the vanilla toffee coming through as the smoke clears.

Verdict

67

Producer
Distillery
Visitor Centre
Availability
Price

Mackmyra Svensk Whisky AB
Mackmyra, Valbo, Sweden
Phone to check tour availability
Specialists and online
⬜⬛⬜⬜⬜

www.mackmyra.com

Mackmyra

One of the really exciting things about the world of whisky in the last decade has been the explosion of new producers, all striving to offer their own distinctive slant on a simple mixture of water, barley and yeast. Some of the offerings have some way to go yet, while some are fascinating, but even the very best of them present a problem for this book: availability. The vast majority of these producers are tiny, boutique operations producing very limited quantities of whisky that tends to sell out very quickly.

Mackmyra is not the only whisky distillery in Sweden, though it was the first, but because it's been around since 1999 there is a chance that you'll be able to track some of it down. Realistically, you'll have to take what you can get (the first release in March 2006 sold out in less than an hour) but that's no hardship.

This is more than a curiosity. There are a number of special editions and limited releases but what you'll probably stumble over is a version of their Preludium (the initial releases from the distillery), but possibly the First Edition might also be seen. All are worth trying: Mackmyra keep experimenting with different casks and finishes, and they even mature their whisky 50 metres underground in an old mine!

You can buy your own cask from the distillery and go and visit it. Be aware, however, that Mackmyra is not inexpensive. Presumably due to high labour costs in Sweden and the fact that all products are bottled at around 46% abv, a bottle typically costs around £50–60 (more for Preludium, which is also in a smaller-than-normal half-litre bottle). Worth it, though.

Colour   Pale gold.
Nose   Fruity with citrus, pear, apple, honey, light oak and cereal notes.
Taste   Citrus, caramel and honey. A light suggestion of oak may be noted.
Finish   Hints of dark chocolate.

Verdict

Producer	Fortune Brands, Inc.
Distillery	Maker's Mark, Loretto, Kentucky
Visitor Centre	Yes
Availability	Some supermarkets and specialists
Price	☐☐☐☐☐

www.makersmark.com

Maker's Mark

This Kentucky bourbon was for some time something of a cult among drinkers on both sides of the Atlantic, driven by the personality of the ebullient Bill Samuels Jr, a direct descendant of the founder. I met him some years ago and it wasn't long before he handed me a gun to look at – an antique as it happened but, for a simple chap like me, it was a somewhat unnerving moment.

It is some years, however, since the distillery was privately owned. Though its marketing likes to give the impression of independence, the company has in fact passed through several corporate hands since 1981 and is today part of Fortune Brands, who also own Jim Beam, Laphroaig and Canadian Club whiskies, among other famous names.

It still appears idiosyncratic, however – uniquely amongst US whiskies styling itself 'whisky' in the Scottish manner; increasing production in 2002 by building a second distillery alongside the first, instead of simply expanding the existing plant; and rotating their barrels within the warehouse levels to achieve more even ageing.

Its appearance is also highly distinctive: a square bottle is capped by red wax, which drips on to the bottle. More importantly, the mash bill recipe does not include any rye, but rather contains exclusively yellow corn, red winter wheat and malted barley. Distillation starts in a column still and is finished in a copper pot still, all of which contribute to the final flavour.

It is particularly appreciated for its comparatively gentle and subtle taste, more mellow than many bourbons. Today, though more widely distributed than when the brand was built, it has maintained something of a reputation as a drinker's drink: one for those 'in the know'. Now that includes you.

Colour Amber.

Nose Vanilla and spice, tropical fruits and some sweet oak wood.

Taste At 45% abv, this is medium to full bodied, with spices (ginger), caramel and a mouth-coating oiliness.

Finish Some smoke, delicately combining with honeyed fruits.

Verdict

69

Producer	Heaven Hill Distilleries, Inc.
Distillery	Bernheim, Louisville, Kentucky
Visitor Centre	Yes
Availability	Specialists
Price	☐☐☐☐☐

www.heaven-hill.com

Mellow Corn

Here's something unusual and uniquely American – the nearest thing you'll get to moonshine that's legal (the Scotch equivalent is 'new make' – see the entry for Glenglassaugh's Spirit Drink). It's far from the nicest whisky you'll drink, at least compared to the others listed here, but it's cheap, fun and worth trying (if only to understand the beneficial influences of malted barley and ageing).

But first, a word of explanation. Before there was bourbon, there was straight corn whiskey. Today, corn whiskey is made with a minimum of 80% of corn in the mash bill and must be matured, if it is matured at all, in uncharred new white oak barrels or refill bourbon barrels. The association is with bootlegging, moonshine and generally depriving the Government of their share, so it represents a deeply rooted American tradition, also expressed in popular culture through NASCAR racing and TV shows such as *The Dukes of Hazzard*.

The production of moonshine still thrives, or so one would deduce from the number of home-made stills and associated equipment to be seen on various internet auction sites but, for a long time, the only mainstream legal producer keeping the tradition alive was Heaven Hill – and good on them, I say. Some smaller craft producers have now joined in the fun.

Heaven Hill actually makes a range, including Dixie Dew and J W Corn, which seems to be the upmarket one! Georgia Moon comes in the kind of jar your granny used to make jam or preserves and is even cheaper (and rawer) than Mellow Corn; the label on this boasts that it's 'aged less than 30 days' which at least is honest.

Unless you want to save a couple of pounds, Mellow Corn is the one to try. It benefits from two years' ageing and comes at a useful 50% abv. Definitely one to serve blind to the whisky snob in your life.

Colour Pale gold.
Nose Waxy (it should be), with lighter floral notes and vanilla.
Taste Surprisingly complex, with mouth-coating oiliness; some fruit and toffee.
Finish Quite lively; the fruit, wood and caramel notes hang on in there.
Verdict

70

Producer	William Grant & Sons Distillers Ltd
Distillery	n/a – this is a blend
Visitor Centre	None – but both Glenfiddich and The Balvenie have tours
Availability	Some supermarkets and specialists
Price	☐☐☐☐☐

www.monkeyshoulder.com

Monkey Shoulder

This isn't really what you'd expect from William Grants, makers of Glenfiddich and The Balvenie. The deliberately funky name (which, as we shall see, has some whisky heritage – but really!); the painfully hip website and the emphasis on cocktails and trendy style bars all smack of an achingly self-conscious marketing strategy.

The thing is, it's pretty decent whisky and it appears to have worked so, as the young people apparently say, 'respect'. So what is it? Technically, it's blended malt – that is to say, a mixture of several single malts but no grain whisky (that would make it an ordinary blend). Being in the fortunate position of owning several distilleries, Grants blended some Glenfiddich, some Balvenie and some Kininvie (a third distillery on their Dufftown site they tend to keep quiet about) to create a whisky designed for easy drinking and use in cocktails.

It was created by their Master Blender David Stewart, as traditional a whisky man as you'll find, and is prepared in small batches of carefully selected casks that then undergo further maturation before bottling.

Rather tongue-in-cheekily I feel, Grants refer to it in their promotional literature as 'triple malt Scotch whisky'. They ought to know better, but we'll let that pass. It has been enthusiastically picked up by a number of rather more cutting-edge bars in those markets where it's been released so far and has collected a few awards.

It's also competitively priced, with fun packaging featuring three monkeys climbing up the neck of the bottle. And the name? It refers to a condition which apparently affected the workers on the malting floor after turning malt by hand. Not, as you might expect, some kind of monkey business.

Find someone who doesn't like whisky and try this on them, perhaps in one of the various cocktails suggested on the brand's website. In fact, go ape!

Colour Bright gold, with copper tints.
Nose Vanilla, lemon zest and fresh fruit.
Taste You'll probably mix it but bananas (no, really), some spice and hints of citrus.
Finish Relaxed and fairly short finish, but holds together well.

Verdict

71

Producer	Diageo
Distillery	Mortlach, Dufftown, Banffshire
Visitor Centre	None
Availability	Specialists
Price	■■■□□

SPEYSIDE
SINGLE MALT
SCOTCH WHISKY

MORTLACH

was the first of seven
distilleries in *Dufftown*. In the
C19th *farm animals* kept in
adjoining byres were fed on
barley left over from processing.
Today *water* from springs in
the *CONVAL HILLS* is used to
produce this delightful
smooth, fruity single
MALT SCOTCH WHISKY

AGED **16** YEARS

43% vol   70 cl

Mortlach

16 Years Old

For reasons which aren't entirely clear, Mortlach never made it into Diageo's Classic Malts selection, probably because the majority of output from the classic Speyside distillery – Dufftown's first – is required for blending, where it is a major component in Johnnie Walker.

It's a shame because there is a lot here to engage whisky fans. We have the distillery's historical significance: built originally in 1823, it was briefly a brewery and even a church, and William Grant was Manager here before starting Glenfiddich. The distillery was entirely remodelled in the 1960s but retained the unorthodox arrangement of the stills. At Mortlach there are three wash stills and three spirit stills. Conventional enough you might think, but all are different sizes and the distillation process, sometimes referred to as 'partial triple distillation', is unique.

In addition, Mortlach has retained its external worm tub condensers and the result, after lengthy maturation, is a big, meaty, full-flavoured whisky that is well liked by those fortunate enough to get a bottle. Sadly, visiting the distillery is difficult as there is no visitor centre and public access is restricted.

There are a number of independent third-party bottlings available and, over the years, Diageo have released some special editions, most recently the Manager's Choice expression (just 240 bottles at £250 for a 12-year-old whisky – little wonder that this exercise was greeted with some scepticism in a few whisky blogging circles).

But it's hardly necessary to splash out to this extent. The standard 16 Years Old bottling will appeal to lovers of substantial, robust whiskies capable of complexity and surprising subtlety (but just imagine if it were offered non-chill filtered at 46% abv). The late Michael Jackson described Mortlach as 'statuesque' and 'elegant', once writing that, 'I find new aromas and flavours every time I raise the glass.' I would not presume to disagree.

Colour Dark and rich, the cask influence is evident.
Nose Immediate sherry cask impact, rich fruit cake aromas, but floral notes also develop.
Taste Rich, meaty and solid; dried fruit and some burnt notes (not unpleasant).
Finish Spice and wood come through with hints of smoke.
Verdict

72

Producer
Distillery

Visitor Centre
Availability
Price

Nikka
Yoichi and Miyagikyo
Distilleries, Japan
Yes at both sites
Specialists
■■□□□

www.nikka.com

Nikka

All Malt

Pay attention: this is very, very interesting and possibly unique. This is a non-aged, blended malt whisky using pot still malt whisky from Nikka's Yoichi and Miyagikyo distilleries and some whisky distilled in a continuous (Coffey) still at Miyagikyo, from a mash comprising 100% malted barley.

So if such a thing was ever made in Scotland the words 'malt whisky' couldn't appear as the Scotch Whisky Association (SWA) have determined that malt whisky cannot be made in a column still, even if the still is entirely made of copper and the mash is 100% malted barley. This has led to some controversy with distillers, such as Loch Lomond (curiously, not members of the SWA) pointing out the illogicality of this position and some commentators suggesting that this is both a bar to innovation and that it suppresses moves towards a greener, more energy-efficient industry.

I am not alone in arguing that this is horribly reminiscent of the attitude of the British manufacturing industry in the 1950s and 1960s when we still made cars, TVs, ships and so on until hidebound management, intransigent trade unions and complacent politicians allowed imports (often from Japan, as it happens) to take over our markets. This is not to adopt a xenophobic 'little Britain' mentality, but simply to observe that all things change; that innovation is the lifeblood of consumer marketing and that hanging on to some self-serving vision of authenticity, traditional practice and heritage (that owes more to marketing spin than historical facts) may well prove something of a blind alley.

But the cumulative wisdom of the Scotch whisky industry disagrees with me and, as was observed as early as 1930, that comprises a body of men well 'assured of their commercial acumen'. Well, we shall see – I shall be happy to be proved wrong.

Anyway, they are not so hidebound in Japan and so we can try and judge for ourselves. This is something of a bargain and delicious in a gentle, self-effacing sort of way.

Colour Rich gold.
Nose Clean, delicate with hints of cereal.
Taste Mouth coating, toffee and vanilla; malty with pear fruit and vanilla development.
Finish Light but consistent and holds together well.
Verdict

73

Producer Diageo
Distillery Oban, Argyll and Bute
Visitor Centre Yes
Availability Specialists and possibly some better supermarkets

Price ■■□□□

www.malts.com

Oban
14 Years Old

This is one of the Diageo Classic Malts range, so it hardly needs promoting here. Yet it always seems to me that this whisky lacks the fame and glamour of some of its stable mates. Perhaps the owners don't promote it as heavily, as production is restricted by Oban's limited scale and stocks would rapidly run out if everyone knew just how good this was.

The distillery lies at the heart of this rather charming West Highland town, which has grown up round it, so much so that it's impossible to see how it could now be expanded. But perhaps that's a good thing, as the character can't be changed by growth and things will go on pretty much as they have in living memory.

There are two 'standard' expressions – at 14 Years Old and the so-called Distiller's Edition, which is finished in sherry casks. There are also occasional special releases such as the Manager's Choice. Frankly, these seem to me rather cynically designed for the collectors' market and there is a growing body of opinion that they might just be a tad over-priced.

But we don't need to worry because it leaves more of the delicious 14-year-old style for us. This is lovely stuff! Bags of complexity, salt and smoke but never unbalanced or over-bearing in delivery; the initial impression is then overtaken by dried fruits and a citric sweetness that fades gently with more smoke and malty notes. Great value at under £40. If you find some of the Islay malts just too much, then you may find this exactly to your taste. Personally, I love it.

Colour Mid gold.
Nose Fresh and clean with a salty tang; some fruit and whiffs of smoke.
Taste Medium body, soft and mouth coating; initially sweet but develops greater complexity with spice, orange, drifting smoke and dries as it evolves.
Finish Is the salty tang imagined by association? Only another glass can answer this conundrum!

Verdict

74

Producer	Inver House Distillers Ltd
Distillery	Old Pulteney, Wick, Caithness
Visitor Centre	Yes
Availability	Specialists and possibly some better supermarkets
Price	▢■■▢▢

www.oldpulteney.com

Old Pulteney

17 Years Old

'When I got of an age to understand Old Pulteney, I could admire its quality when well matured, recognising in it some of the strong characteristics of the northern temperament.' So observed one of Scotland's finest writers and whisky's most ardent champions, Neil M. Gunn, in his 1935 classic *Whisky & Scotland* (try and read it one day).

Well, Old Pulteney is still possessed of a singular character and nowhere is this expressed more remarkably and forcefully than in this 17 Year Old expression. This distillery is located on the coast at Wick and makes much play of its coastal location and the curious flat-topped stills. It has changed hands on a number of occasions during its long life but, today, seems to be really valued by its owners Inver House. They have worked hard to promote the brand and have released a number of interesting expressions, including a venerable 30 Years Old.

But, for its combination of exceptional taste and real value, I'd have to pick their 17 Years Old (there is a 21-year-old version, but it seems to me just a trifle over-aged). To tell the truth, if this teenager was on Islay, whisky fans would be fighting to get it, savouring the piquant, salty taste and the long, lingering finish. Some tasters pick up pineapple and coconut notes, while others praise the sweet/salt balance. Personally, I love the saltiness which then gives way to vanilla and a deliciously creamy, mouth-filling (it's bottled at 46% abv), slightly sweet orange, before fading away gently.

This has won a number of significant awards in the last few years – the judges certainly knew what they were doing. Neil Gunn would love it and he was a fine judge of whisky.

Colour Very pale for the age, but predominantly matured in ex-bourbon wood.

Nose Sweet and yet salty; loads of honey, vanilla and lemon.

Taste Remarkably complex and justifies taking time over it; malted barley notes roll over into some liquorice and chocolate flavours, with a steady drumbeat of salt ever present.

Finish Goes on and on, drying and fading steadily and consistently.

Verdict

75

Producer	Irish Distillers
Distillery	Midleton, Cork, Ireland
Visitor Centre	Yes
Availability	Specialists and possibly some better supermarkets
Price	☐■☐☐☐

www.irishdistillers.ie

Redbreast

Let's assume that you couldn't find any Green Spot (no particular surprise). This is what you need to get – not that this is in any way second best and, at 12 years of age, it has some additional maturity to show off. Again, this is an Irish pot still whiskey and thus something of a rarity, though you will find Redbreast a little easier to track down than the elusive Green Spot.

Irish Distillers is today part of the giant Pernod Ricard group and they take their distilling very seriously. You can visit the distillery near Cork, though what you see is actually a museum and visitor centre, albeit a very good one, in the old distillery which no longer produces. The real work goes on just out of sight at a modern plant with a remarkable range of stills, producing all kinds of spirit (including gin and vodka). Needless to say, you don't get to see that.

Redbreast was originally produced in 1939 for Gilbey's by the original Jameson distillery. But after that closed, stocks of maturing whiskey ran out and the brand was withdrawn. Observing the refusal of Green Spot to die and the upsurge in single malt Scotch, Irish Distillers brought it back as a 12-year-old from Midleton, to general acclaim. A mix of both sherry and bourbon casks go into the blend and the full-on style is a classic of its type.

This is a major award winner and always scores highly in independent tastings. Great value at under £30.

Colour A subtle bronzed gold.
Nose Tons of body on the nose, promising excitement within!
Taste A massive whiskey, but with plenty going on and layers of flavour to explore. Sweet, with lots of ripe fruit and spice notes. Honeyed brioche. Very full and oily for a 40% abv.
Finish Stick with it for waves of vanilla, honey, oak and spice.

Verdict

76

Producer
Distillery
Visitor Centre
Availability

Price

Chivas Brothers Ltd
Scapa, Orkney
No
Specialists and possible
duty free
▪▪▪☐☐

www.chivasbrothers.com see also www.scapamalt.com

SCAPA
'the' ORCADIAN

Single Malt SCOTCH WHISKY
FROM THE SANCTUARY OF THE SCAPA FLOW

YRS **16** OLD
40% vol 70cl

from the ISLANDS of ORKNEY
A SMOOTH & FULL BODIED SINGLE MALT
ESTᴰ 1885

Scapa

14/16 Years Old

Dramatically located on Orkney's famous Scapa Flow, the little Scapa distillery has suffered from turbulent history, inconsistent marketing and the dominant shadow of its more famous neighbour Highland Park. It's still worth paying attention to this little gem, however. You have to be careful what you buy, though, and to appreciate that you have to understand some of the history.

By 2004 Scapa presented a doleful appearance; much of the roof was missing, and the electrical system out of action and it was generally assumed that it was doomed. However, to general surprise, over £2m was then spent on a complete refurbishment – though it remains firmly closed to the public. The following year Pernod Ricard's Chivas Brothers acquired the distillery and, again, there were rumours of closure or possibly disposal.

Hope, though, sprang up among lovers of this ugly duckling – perhaps a swan would emerge after all. For some years, a 14-year-old expression had been marketed in a desultory fashion, but it was appreciated by connoisseurs wanting to explore a lighter, unpeated island style that was quite unique. However, Chivas relaunched the brand and a 16-year-old expression was released – sadly, not in my view a great triumph.

The price shot up and for that you get a rather more elegant bottle and box but the whisky is something of an anticlimax. Because there was insufficient stock to go round all their world markets, the decision was taken to bottle at 40% abv. Mistake. It's rather thin (chill filtered to boot) and lacks real distinction, though it's perfectly pleasant, with some honey flavours and a salty bite. What's more, I think you can ignore all the marketing-speak on the website about the Lomond wash still: in my view it isn't. It's been heavily modified and, with its internal plates removed, it's simply a pot still with a rather unusual head and neck. So there!

So no tasting notes here because I don't know which whisky you're going to find. What you really need to do is find a merchant bottling and cross your fingers it's a good one – the Gordon & MacPhail and Provenance versions have attracted some praise.

I suppose, feeling charitable, you could buy the official version if only to encourage them. They have tried, after all, to do the right thing and it's a big improvement on the last lot's feeble efforts.

Verdict

77

Producer	The Spencerfield Spirits Company
Distillery	n/a – this is a blend of various malts produced by Whyte & Mackay
Visitor Centre	n/a
Availability	Specialists and possibly some better supermarkets
Price	■■□□□

www.spencerfieldspirit.com

Sheep Dip

God loves a trier, or so they say. Well, Spencerfield Spirits are certainly trying.

The company was formed when Alex Nicol, then at Whyte & Mackay but with a long industry career, fell out with his bosses and left. Nothing unusual there but, in place of the usual severance package, he took with him the rights to the unloved Sheep Dip brand, which was then languishing in the corporate cellars, and signed a supply agreement for whisky.

Then he convinced W&M's Master Blender, the ebullient Richard Paterson, to work with him and together they created a new blended malt for Sheep Dip. Back in the day, Sheep Dip had been a cult success, but it relied on independent ownership to give the brand and its customers the necessary time and attention. In corporate hands it just wasn't a priority and it slowly faded away.

Alex and his wife Jane have changed all that. Having got the whisky right they invested in some dramatic new packaging and an old horse box, which they drive round various country fairs sampling the product and selling bottles. Slowly but surely, it's gathering a new following and once people try a bottle they want more. And so Sheep Dip is slowly and painfully, bottle by bottle, getting back on its feet.

I wouldn't tell you all this if it wasn't also very good whisky. It's a great story and a great whisky from some great people (Alex: will that do?). Oh, and they have a great website, as well, which tells you all this in so much more loving detail.

Colour Rich, warming gold.
Nose Quite floral with honey, malt and fresh fruits.
Taste Dominated by solid Highland and Speyside malts, this has plenty of weight without lacking subtlety or balance.
Finish Lots to look for as the Islay component finally kicks in, adding smoke; some spice lingers also.

Verdict

78

Producer	Ian Macleod Distillers Ltd
Distillery	n/a
Visitor Centre	n/a
Availability	Specialists
Price	▣▣▣▣☐

www.smokehead.co.uk

Smokehead
Extra Black

Aargh! This is one of those 'Ronseal' whiskies: it does exactly what it says on the chunky tin. I don't really like it but, if your taste runs to big, peaty, smoky monsters then you need to try it. Frankly, I find it all a bit too much, but I can't deny it's a roller-coaster of a dram. Actually, it's more of a weapon of mass destruction – to my taste buds at least. I needed a good night's sleep before the palate was clear and the work of tasting could continue.

For that reason, be warned – this takes no prisoners. It's an 18-year-old Islay single malt (unspecified, but one of the extreme ones) bottled by the excellent Ian Macleod Distillers to take advantage of the current vogue for peaty whisky. I can't imagine what else they'd use this for: the tiniest drop in a blending vat and the taste would dominate the finished product.

There is a little brother, the regular Smokehead. But if you like this kind of thing, why bother with the monkey, when you can have the organ grinder? I saw Extra Black compared to the amplifier that goes all the way up to 11 in *Spinal Tap*. This is just as rock and roll as that. And as pointless, really, unless 11 is where you want to go.

I'll leave it up to you. You have been warned. And it's not particularly cheap either. But that's rock and roll for you.

Colour Curiously pale. I don't think this has ever seen the inside of a sherry cask.

Nose Peat, smoke, more smoke, more peat. Salt. Then peat.

Taste Explosions of spice, pepper and, yes, peat smoke. Just huge waves of peat. And salt.

Finish Excuse me, I have to leave now and get a glass of water.

Verdict

79

Producer	Inver House Distillers Ltd
Distillery	Speyburn, Rothes, Banffshire
Visitor Centre	No
Availability	Specialists
Price	☐☐☐■☐

www.speyburn.com

Speyburn
Solera 25 Years Old

A little-known but traditional and very attractive Speyside distillery, Speyburn deserves wider fame. The 10-year-old style enjoys some success in the USA, as much because of aggressive pricing as anything else, but you hardly see it in the UK, which is a great shame. And no visitor centre either, also a shame.

Another classic Charles Doig design, the distillery was built in 1897 at the end of the great Victorian whisky boom, and for years was part of the DCL. They first mothballed it in response to the over-production of the 1980s (the so-called 'whisky loch') but thankfully sold it to Airdrie-based Inver House Distillers in 1991.

Most of the spirit goes for blending but the distillery offer the spectacular 25-year-old Solera expression which is, as the saying goes, 'to die for'. It is quite remarkably good. In fact, I don't really think they know how good it is, because you can find a bottle in UK specialists at around £70, which is just silly.

But don't tell them – just snap up a bottle or three and enjoy a rich, luscious, classic Speysider at a tasty 46% abv which, with a better-known name and some sexy designer packaging, would have whisky fans queuing round the block to give three figures for a bottle of it. In fact, if you poured this into a bottle of— We'd better not explore that thought any further!

Suffice it to say this is a very well-kept secret. You can't visit the distillery (shame) and bottles are hard to find but I promise you'll be impressed. Get some before anyone tells the owners.

Colour Curiously pale for the age, but an attractive light gold.
Nose Soft oak and vanilla. Honey, fruit cake and some light smoke.
Taste Mouth coating, rich and warm; buttered honey sweetness, burnt orange and delicate oak notes.
Finish Smooth, well-balanced and consistent. Maybe a hint of dark orange, just at the end.

Verdict

80

Producer	J & A Mitchell & Co. Ltd
Distillery	Springbank, Campbeltown, Argyll and Bute
Visitor Centre	Yes
Availability	Specialists
Price	☐☐☐☐☐

www.springbankwhisky.com

Springbank
10 Years Old

Once upon a time the town of Campbeltown was one of the most important and respected distilling centres in Scotland. But, over the years and for a variety of reasons, it declined until only one really active distillery was left – Springbank.

It struggled on during the 1970s and 1980s as something of an anachronism, a historical curiosity, quirky, stubbornly independent and almost wilfully resistant to change. In 1987 the late Michael Jackson recorded that its 'very traditional plant has not produced for some years'.

However, there were always a few die-hard enthusiasts and keepers of the true flame and the owners resolutely soldiered on, oblivious to 'progress'. In those days you could buy your own cask but, sadly, they won't let you do that any more. As the single malt boom gathered pace in the early 1990s, Springbank began to acquire a cult, almost mythic, status greatly enhanced by its remote location (even by Scottish standards Campbeltown is awkward to reach) and the distillery's hermit-like reluctance to embrace publicity.

The plant is still traditional – in fact, walking round the distillery is like stepping into a Victorian distilling textbook – and Springbank adheres to an unusual 2½ times distillation process (there is a very good explanation on their website, so I'm not even going to try). This and the floor malting, lack of chill filtration or colouring and labour-intensive production mean that Springbank is arguably the most traditional of Scotch whisky.

In recent years it has flourished and the owners have even been so bold as to open a new distillery, Kilkerran. A variety of styles are produced at Springbank and they vary dramatically (see entry for Longrow) but this is the standard and most widely available. A 'must have' whisky if there ever was one.

Colour	This has been known to vary according to the casks they use from pale gold to a darker shade. Don't worry – it's just part of the idiosyncratic fun.
Nose	Expect leather, some peat smoke hints, spices and a salty note.
Taste	More saltiness, nutmeg and cinnamon, orange peel and, bizarrely, vinegar. But nice.
Finish	Slightly perfumed with a sweet/salt tussle going on. Hints of smoke linger at the end.
Verdict	

81

Producer The English Whisky Co.
Distillery St George's Distillery,
Roudham, Norfolk

Visitor Centre Yes
Availability Specialists
Price ■■□□□

www.englishwhisky.co.uk

St George's

I'm taking a small gamble here and assuming that by the time this gets into bookshops the initial hype and excitement surrounding English whisky will have worn off and products will be available once again. For, at the time of writing, St George's have been so swamped by orders that they have sold out of their first whisky and have suspended their online shop.

The distillery was founded by James and Andrew Nelstrop, Norfolk farmers, and began distilling in November 2006 with the legendary Iain Henderson (from Islay) in charge. Unlike some other people's more speculative projects, the Nelstrops were able to finance the development from their own resources and, as a result, progress on the distillery was rapid.

They have taken the admirable step of not pre-selling whisky until they were actually in production, as opposed to some other would-be distillery promoters. Indeed, Andrew Nelstrop takes a strong line on this, commenting that: 'flogging casks before you've built the distillery is a crime,' as he told the 2009 World Whiskies Conference. I, for one, think he's right. If you're tempted to 'invest' in such a scheme go and lie down for a while until the mood passes!

English whisky is not actually new. There were whisky distilleries in England in the 1800s but they all closed by the turn of the century. With excellent quality barley on hand, first-rate equipment and a very positive attitude there is no reason why St George's can't flourish and, indeed, become the first of many English whisky distilleries.

There is an excellent visitor centre at Roudham (some people actually plan to get married there) and you can tour the distillery and taste a range of products, from new make spirit to, by the time you read this, four-year-old whisky. It's definitely a venture to support – innovative, hand-crafted and highly individual, this is the kind of thing that brings much-needed variety, excitement and interest to the whisky scene.

Initial impressions of the new make and the first release of a three-year-old whisky in December 2009 were very positive so it seems safe to suggest you can buy with confidence.

Verdict

82

Producer	Diageo
Distillery	Talisker, Skye
Visitor Centre	Yes
Availability	Specialists and possibly some better supermarkets
Price	■■□□□

ESTD 1830

TALISKER

THE ONLY SINGLE MALT SCOTCH WHISKY
FROM THE ISLE OF SKYE

From the western shores of the Isle of Skye, in the lofty shadow of the Cuillin Hills, comes a single malt like no other. Its strong and full-bodied spirit, with a warming afterglow, is easy to enjoy yet, like Skye itself, so hard to leave.

AGED **10** YEARS

45.8% vol

SINGLE MALT SCOTCH WHISKY
TALISKER DISTILLERY CARBOST ISLE OF SKYE

70cl

www.malts.com

Talisker
10 Years Old

Another of the Classic Malts range from Diageo, Talisker has long been praised for its brazen, up-front, uncompromising flavours. Like a number of the recommendations here, it's a very forceful product indeed.

Personally, they're not my favourites but it's hard to deny that lots of people like them and, once they try this style, absolutely fall in love with it – all the more so, in this case, if you visit the distillery (and you should try to).

Out of the various different releases I'd recommend the 'standard' 10 Years Old as an introduction to Talisker, and then you can move on to the 18 Years Old (see next entry).

Talisker has long had its fans: in 1880 Robert Louis Stevenson listed it as one of the three 'king o'drinks' and in his seminal and highly influential book *Whisky* (1930) Aeneas MacDonald had Talisker wrestling with Clynelish for inclusion in his list of the twelve most distinguished of Highland whiskies.

Today the distillery runs along quite traditional lines. It still uses wooden worm tubs and, uniquely, the lyne arms on the wash stills are designed to trap vapours from the first distillation before they reach the outside worm tubs, while a small secondary copper pipe carries the trapped vapours back to the wash stills for a second distillation. Also traditionally, and commendably, Talisker is bottled at higher strength (here 45.8% abv) just to add to the fun.

If the distillation sounds complicated, it's because it is, but all this has a huge, if not fully understood, influence on flavour: the result has to be experienced to be completely appreciated. Once tasted never forgotten.

Colour Bright gold.

Nose Assertive marine character with waves of smoke.

Taste Surprises with some sweetness, then fruits, smoke and seaweed take over. Some commentators recommend trying it with seafood – oysters or good smoked salmon seem to work.

Finish Lots to give here with the sweetness coming back and a distinctive sharp pepper bite.

Verdict

83

Producer	Diageo
Distillery	Talisker, Skye
Visitor Centre	Yes
Availability	Specialists and possibly some better supermarkets
Price	☐■☐☐☐

www.malts.com

Talisker
18 Years Old

As I have said, I personally find this style of whisky rather overwhelming. Great for after dinner, perhaps, or drunk out of doors, but just too much like hard work to drink on its own or when a 'quiet dram' is called for. I have a personal theory that there's a large element of fashion at work here – but I've beaten that drum elsewhere and, to stretch that metaphor, there's no doubt I'm out of step and marching to a different tune.

So, another Talisker, because I don't for a moment deny its greatness. Moving up from the 'standard' 10 Years Old we encounter this beastie. It's been widely praised by enthusiasts and was chosen as 'Best Whisky in the World 2007' in the World Whiskies Awards. I don't hold with such hyperbole (it wouldn't be my personal best, in any event) but it does indicate the esteem in which this dram is held.

Mind you, on a well-known merchant's site I saw a consumer contribute a tasting note which read 'tastes like combing your hair'. This may well be a first. I am still struggling to work out what was meant.

Diageo has worked hard with Talisker, exploiting its distinctive taste and its unique position as Skye's only distillery (there are tentative plans for a farmhouse competitor but, while that's a wonderful idea, if you ask me, it will never happen). As well as the 10- and 18-year-old styles suggested here, there are a number of more expensive special editions, limited releases and occasional distillery exclusive bottlings, which make the journey over the sea to Skye all the more pleasurable.

And, if you resell on eBay to the collectors, it can be profitable. Not that I would recommend that for a moment, you understand, not even for a prince's ransom.

Colour Deeper than its younger brother.
Nose Everything you wanted but more! More smoke! More peat! More fruits! Just more!
Taste Toffee, peat and wood, of course, but well balanced with the citrus fruitiness and lingering sweet notes. Bacon and orange marmalade.
Finish Waves of flavour give way to the trademark Talisker pepper kick.

Verdict

Producer
Distillery
Visitor Centre

Availability

Price

William Grant & Sons Distillers Ltd
Balvenie, Dufftown, Banffshire
Yes – but booking in advance
is necessary
Specialists and possibly some
better supermarkets
▣▣▣▣☐

www.thebalvenie.com

The Balvenie

PortWood 21 Years Old

The Balvenie is the little brother to Glenfiddich and, for some years, has been rather unfairly overshadowed by its stable mate (almost literally, as it happens, as the distillery lies just below the Glenfiddich site).

More recently, however, Grants have understood the quality offered by The Balvenie and promoted it more actively with a growing range of releases. The distillery is characterised by maintaining a floor malting, one of the last in Scotland, and may be acquitted of the charge of keeping this on solely for its tourist value by the fact that, until even more recently, it was closed to the public.

However, you can now take an excellent tour which, though superficially expensive, in fact offers great insight into production at The Balvenie and culminates with an extensive tasting of older whiskies, making it very good value. Numbers are limited so it is essential to book in advance. Concentrating on the whisky, the usual clichéd audio-visual presentation is absent (which only enhances the pleasure).

There are a range of expressions and styles but my favourite is the 21-year-old PortWood finish. Some of these finishes can be overdone and the whisky spoiled by an unsubtle use of the second wood, but this was created by the hand of a master. Delicate port wine flavours dance round the inherent spirit quality in a mesmerising and quite beguiling fashion.

David Stewart, Grants' Master Blender, has spent longer than he probably cares to admit in the industry and is widely respected by his peers. For me, this is a stellar achievement, fully justifying his high reputation.

Colour Warm highlights in rich gold.
Nose Raisins and nuts; continues to develop a well-rounded sweetness over time.
Taste Silky and full bodied, the port casks seduce but never swamp the underlying spirit character.
Finish Lingers very nicely and continues to offer a well-mannered, nutty memory.

Verdict

85

Producer   William Grant & Sons Distillers Ltd
Distillery   Balvenie, Dufftown, Banffshire
Visitor Centre   Yes – but booking in advance
                      is necessary
Availability   Specialists and possibly some
                      better supermarkets
Price   ⬜🟦🟦🟦🟦

www.thebalvenie.com

The Balvenie

30 Years Old

If you like older whisky, prefer the Speyside style and don't require lavish packaging, then this might well be a good choice.

The spirit here would have been distilled in the late 1970s just as the infamous 'whisky loch' was filling up. For those of a historical turn of mind, this was a period of disastrous over-production at a time of falling sales, which resulted in draconian distillery closures and the ensuing loss of some famous names, such as Port Ellen and St Magdalene in Linlithgow. This episode is regretted to this day and has left enduring scars on the Scotch whisky industry.

However, while hardly immune from broader economic conditions, prudently managed, privately owned companies are not as driven by the short-term diktats of the stock market as their publicly quoted brethren, nor do they live in constant fear of being swallowed up by a larger rival. As a result, they can quietly carry on laying down stock (so long as they can pay for it) in the knowledge that whisky has a long history of boom and bust and that, eventually, the carefully husbanded casks will acquire the status of liquid gold.

There is currently a trend for some companies to release beautifully packaged but expensive non-aged whiskies, arguing that the benefits of ageing are over-stated and that quality of blending is all – younger whiskies add vibrancy, and all that. While there is some truth in this, it's also a fact that the industry cut production so drastically in the early to mid 1980s that many firms simply don't have any old whisky to sell – call me cynical if you will, but this may partly explain their almost miraculous conversion to the 'non-aged' camp!

Fortunately, the cautious Grant family kept steadily on and today we can enjoy this splendidly mature Balvenie at a cracking 47.3% abv. Expect to pay more than £300 for a bottle but it's worth it. Drink to 'independence' as you sip a dram.

Colour Rich, dark gold.
Nose Initially powdery, but develops a rich complexity with honey notes.
Taste Dried fruits, orange peel, vanilla and Christmas cake spices.
Finish Rolls on to finish with a gentle burst of honey.

Verdict

86

Producer Whyte & Mackay Ltd
Distillery Dalmore, Alness, Ross-shire
Visitor Centre Yes
Availability Widespread international availability

Price ☐☐☐☐☐

www.thedalmore.com

The Dalmore

12 Years Old

I find myself quite conflicted about The Dalmore and its somewhat vulgar and ostentatious claim to be the most expensive malt whisky in the world (a bottle of their 62 Years Old sold once for £32,000). They have quite a few high-priced and ritzy expressions, though high-priced whisky ain't necessarily great whisky. However, there are enough buyers out there who confuse price with quality to ensure that the whisky industry will keep producing these 'luxury' offerings. After all, the only reason that we now have whiskies at £10,000 a bottle is that there are people ready and willing to pay £10,000 for a bottle. But, let's be clear: these are trophies, not whiskies as most of us understand the term.

Dalmore has somehow managed to muscle in on this very top-end market, previously the exclusive preserve of brands like The Macallan, even claiming that some of their products have 'an investment value'. This seems to me to be playing with fire and when I see the Dalmore website using language such as 'alchemistic artistry' and 'dynamic distillation' to describe their production process my scepticism grows. This type of marketing risks losing touch with reality, let alone an informed audience who actually care about whisky.

However, though the marketing boys and girls at Dalmore may have been drinking their own bath water you don't have to: there are still some decent whiskies underneath all their breathless incantations and mumbo-jumbo. Put all the hype to one side and look no further than the entry-level offering at 12 years old. A 50/50 blend of sherry and bourbon casks, this is a textbook example of balance, weight and complexity that offers great value for money.

You could always pour it into a crystal decanter for when the boss comes round.

Colour A lovely warm gold.
Nose Sweet, appetising and calling to you.
Taste Well-balanced sherry and vanilla; dark oranges, spices and dark fruit cake.
Finish Gently fades with a hint of nuts and caramel.

Verdict

87

Producer	Chivas Brothers Ltd
Distillery	Glenlivet, Ballindalloch, Banffshire
Visitor Centre	Yes
Availability	Different expressions widely available
Price	☐☐☐☐☐

www.glenlivet.com

The Glenlivet
21 Years Old Archive

Glenlivet make much play in their marketing of the claim 'the single malt that started it all'. Like most marketing claims, there's some truth in there, but perhaps somewhat embellished. This statement refers to the assertion that the distillery's founder George Smith was the first licensed distiller under an important 1823 Act of Parliament. Well, so what exactly? Since then the distillery has been expanded beyond recognition and production methods have evolved more than a little.

Smith's Glenlivet was always a by-word for quality, though, and not for nothing is this particular whisky allowed to style itself 'The' Glenlivet. So I think he'd probably still be proud of the whisky produced under his name, though what he'd make of its French ownership it might be kinder not to speculate.

The Glenlivet style is characterised by what is generally identified as a 'pineapple' note and that has been highly prized by blenders and drinkers for more than a hundred years. With the older styles, that fruit note can still be detected but the whisky has greater richness and subtlety. The impact of extra ageing and wood quality can be seen in deeper flavours of chocolate, fruit cake, dried fruits and then some engaging and complex spice notes, which, for me, are a hallmark of older Glenlivets and a real stamp of quality and drinking satisfaction.

I could easily have included more than one Glenlivet in this list, but they are widely available (especially in the USA) and so I will do no more than remind you that this is a very great whisky, not to be disregarded on account of its relative ubiquity, thus leaving space for equally fine but more obscure drams.

Colour Pale copper.
Nose Panacotta, ripe plums, dark orange and Christmas cake.
Taste Prunes, subtle coconut; rich and full-bodied with fruity tones. Add water slowly.
Finish Long, rolling flavours holding together well for an extended finish.

Verdict

88

Producer	The Edrington Group
Distillery	Glenrothes, Rothes, Speyside
Visitor Centre	No
Availability	Specialists and possibly some better supermarkets
Price	■■□□□

www.theglenrothes.com

The Glenrothes
Select Reserve

Don't make the mistake of confusing this splendid Speyside single malt with the rather drab and utilitarian new town of the same name in Fife: this is anything but! In fact, it's tucked away off the main street of Rothes in Speyside on the edge of the Rothes burn but, since they don't have any public visitor facilities, the location is fairly academic. The distillery is owned by The Edrington Group but the brand belongs to Berry Bros & Rudd, of St James' in London.

For years, this was a straightforward production unit making a well-respected whisky that was highly demanded for blending: Cutty Sark and The Famous Grouse, among others, rely on The Glenrothes. In fact, despite expanding the distillery twice, demand was so great that there was little or no stock left for sale as a single malt. However, in 1987 the first tentative steps were taken and seven years later Berry Bros & Rudd hit on the idea of releasing vintages (perhaps not an unduly radical step for a wine merchant).

Since then, The Glenrothes has gone on to considerable success and some of the vintage bottles fetch fancy prices. But, as a starting point, you can do a lot worse than the Select Reserve, a non-vintage bottling of The Glenrothes which typifies the distillery house character – ripe fruits, citrus, vanilla and hints of spice – and is a fine representative of the classic Speyside style. It's non-aged but the point here is the delivery of consistent character.

The Glenrothes is the antithesis of the classic Islay style, so if you want smoky, peaty whisky this isn't for you. However, for a gentle, subtle and intriguing dram that keeps on giving, look no further. Great whisky at a great price.

Colour Pale gold.
Nose Lashings of vanilla and oak; plums and ripe mango; hints of spice. Sweet.
Taste Well-rounded on the palate, with great balance and style. Dried fruits, citrus notes and slightly floral.
Finish A creamy finish with subtle spice notes toward the end.

Verdict

89

Producer	Highland Distillers Ltd
Distillery	Macallan, Craigellacchie, Speyside
Visitor Centre	Yes – booking in advance is necessary for the better tours
Availability	Specialists and possibly some better supermarkets
Price	☐■☐☐☐

www.themacallan.com

The Macallan
Sherry Oak 10 Years Old

The Macallan was an early pioneer in single malt, earning itself the sobriquet 'the Rolls-Royce of single malts', on which description it has been dining out ever since. And not without good reason for, if you like this style, it is very, very good.

But hold on, you cry – what style is that? Your confusion is understandable. For years, The Macallan made great play of their exclusive use of sherry barrels for ageing their whisky, then in November 2004 they launched their Fine Oak range, which didn't. Initially, purists were outraged but The Macallan has had the last laugh as their sales have been highly impressive ever since – in fact, this is consistently one of the fastest-growing single malts there is, so presumably they're doing something right. Recently, because they were doing so well, they re-opened a mothballed still house with some rather attractive displays for you to study.

This, then, is the 'standard' expression (at least in the UK; internationally the 12 Years Old is the norm) and a benchmark for the sherry-aged style. The Macallan go to great pains to select and control the wood for their barrels and it shows: this is rich, dark and full-bodied but never oppressive.

It's worth making the trip to the distillery to see the impressive exhibition on wood, which details the forestry, cooperage and warehousing practice that goes into The Macallan. Today there are a bewildering number of expressions and any number of limited releases (some, I suspect, just for the collector) but this is the flagship and a great place to start exploring this grand old malt that has done so much to build understanding and appreciation of fine whisky.

Colour Deep, natural colour from sherry cask ageing.
Nose Immediate sweetness, malt and toffee.
Taste Full bodied but graceful and well-balanced; this is a classic sherry finish.
Finish The sweetness comes through with citrus notes, hints of smoke and oak.

Verdict

90

Producer	Highland Distillers Ltd
Distillery	Macallan, Craigellacchie, Speyside
Visitor Centre	Yes – booking in advance is necessary for the better tours
Availability	Specialists and possibly some better supermarkets
Price	■■■□□

www.themacallan.com

The Macallan
Sherry Oak 18 Years Old

As a quick glance around the shelves of any decent specialist retailer will confirm, there are quite a few different Macallans and it can get confusing. The first thing to get clear is whether you prefer the traditional sherry style or the newer Fine Oak – both are very good but very different. Once you get this sorted out you can become the sort of whisky bore who sends people to sleep at parties.

This is in the original Macallan style – with lashings of sherry on the nose and palate due to the huge impact of the sherry casks. You can read all about this on the Macallan website or even make a pilgrimage to the distillery where they have an exhibition on the subject. A few years ago it would have been fair to say that the quality of these older Macallans was variable (I remember with a shudder sampling a particularly rubbery 25 year old) – under the previous owners there wasn't quite the care and attention lavished on wood selection as there is today.

Now, virtually all Macallan expressions are eagerly consumed by their worldwide legion of fans. The marketing increasingly tries to position Macallan as a 'luxury icon', whatever that may be, but for me this is just a very fine whisky for drinking with like-minded friends after a big dinner. If they're not friends to start with, they should be after you've served this.

However, read on – there are more Macallans to try and to buy, though we're going to steer clear of the super-premium 'editions' and the more lavishly packaged one-off specials. They're largely for collectors and Premier League footballers. We're nearly at the end but don't forget – this is a book for whisky lovers.

Colour Dramatic dark mahogany – rich and deep.
Nose Approach with care – this is very full-on with dramatic notes of wood and leather.
Taste Powerful sherry impact, wine notes, some smoke, chewy vanilla fudge with spicy layers offering up Olde English marmalade and dried fruits.
Finish Very round and consistent. Some smoke hints and classic cake notes.

Verdict

91

Producer	Highland Distillers Ltd
Distillery	Macallan, Craigellacchie, Speyside
Visitor Centre	Yes – booking in advance is necessary for the better tours
Availability	Specialists
Price	▫▫▫◼◼

www.themacallan.com

The Macallan

Fine Oak 30 Years Old

This is as far as we're going with The Macallan and it is the one representative from the Fine Oak range that I've picked. It might be more economically prudent to start with its 10 Years Old little brother (it's about 1/10 of the price for one thing), or the stunning 15 Years Old, but you won't regret splashing out on a bottle of this beauty.

For one thing, it wears its age very lightly and is almost effervescent on the palate, all the more so with a splash of water. That may seem strange (it is, in fact, strange so I tried a second sample on another day with the same result) but I rather like it. What it shows very clearly is the basic integrity and underlying quality of The Macallan spirit without the usual sherry effect.

There's a lot of body here with complex toffee and vanilla and layers of wood and spice. It does demand some concentration and effort on your part, but the effort will be rewarded with a memorable tour through a veritable forest of oak. But it never dominates or overwhelms and that is this whisky's great charm. The distillers described this as having 'a rich, exotic, heady and aromatic nose – reminiscent of an orange grove' but, while there is some sweetness there, I associate the citric note more with the 21 Years Old or the considerably more expensive 1824.

Whatever. Just be careful when you get this out and who you offer it to. It's all too easy to drink and forget the price tag (it'll set you back just over £300 in the UK).

I can't recommend too many whiskies at this level but this is very hard to resist.

Colour Markedly paler than its counterparts; an attractive yellow gold.

Nose Toffee, vanilla, oak and some smoke hints.

Taste Exceptionally complex, rich and mouth coating; black cherry. Lively with water.

Finish Quite creamy, soft and lingering. Layered and sophisticated.

Verdict

92

Producer
Distillery
Visitor Centre
Availability

Price

The Wine Society
n/a – this is a blend
n/a
The Wine Society –
Members' List and website
▨☐☐☐☐

THE SOCIETY'S
Special Highland
Blend
SCOTCH WHISKY
The Wine Society, Stevenage · Product of Scotland

100 cl e   40% vol

www.thewinesociety.com

The Wine Society

Special Highland Blend

Pay attention – this is a serious, under-rated and little-known bargain. First you have to join The Wine Society. Once upon a time this was a sort of upper-class rite of passage, like putting your children down for Eton, getting elected to the MCC or ordering your 12-bore from Purdeys. No longer – they've democratised the Society and you can join online (though their label still looks pretty good in an under-stated sort of a way at smart dinner parties).

Obviously, they mainly sell wine (and great value it is) but hidden away on their list is this little beauty. The Society has had their own blend for years, laying down new fillings in their own sherry casks and waiting a remarkable 14 years until it's ready. Until recently, Edrington's John Ramsay was in charge of the blend and, prudently, considerable stocks have been laid down following his recent retirement so the quality is assured for some years ahead. Only a private members' organisation could do this.

The blend is around 40% single malt, with the delicious, meaty, full-bodied Speysider Mortlach at its heart. Though this is not an Edrington distillery it has, in fact, featured in The Society's Special Highland Blend for many years. The fastidious Society insist that no caramel is used to colour the whisky but, despite the Highland name, I detect some Islay content in the blend – or perhaps the mighty Talisker finds its way in there. After all, the label features a handsome illustration of Dunvegan Castle on Skye, in honour of the Society's first Chairman, the splendidly named The Macleod of Macleod.

Whatever the exact blend recipe, you'll go a long way before you beat this discreetly chic, understated and mellow dram. Excellent value, and their other private label whiskies are also well worth exploring.

Colour Mid gold.
Nose Sherry impact evident and suggestions of age. Some smoke behind.
Taste Very full bodied; a robust and 'solid' whisky, meaty and oily even at 40% abv.
Finish A lingering sweetness remains and plays with faint smoke traces.

Verdict

93

Producer
Distillery
Visitor Centre
Availability
Price

Compass Box Whisky Company
n/a – this is a blending house
n/a
Specialists
☐☐☐☐☐

www.compassboxwhisky.com

The Spice Tree

This is a somewhat controversial whisky. The first release of The Spice Tree inserted brand new oak staves in the casks used to mature the whisky. For reasons too arcane and lengthy to go into here, this attracted the wrath of the Scotch Whisky Association (SWA) who threatened Compass Box with legal action if they didn't stop. The ensuing publicity meant that the whisky sold out in record time but Compass Box felt they couldn't risk any further batches made in this way.

However, they were not deterred and spent the next three years trying to find a maturation method that was within the rules but gave the same effect. This is the result. Instead of inserting staves into the cask, the cask ends themselves have been heavily toasted and the whisky matured for a further two years. (There is a detailed and very clear explanation of this on the Compass Box website.)

It's not immediately evident what the SWA objected to exactly, other than maintaining that the process was not 'traditional'. This opens up a wider debate, with a number of commentators (including me) suggesting that the SWA has a somewhat elastic definition of tradition and that, as a result, it seems that much needed innovation risks being stifled. Producers as diverse as Loch Lomond, Bruichladdich and Compass Box have all taken issue with the SWA's interpretation of the Scotch Whisky regulations, so far to absolutely no avail.

However, this whisky seems to be acceptable to the grand panjandrums and we can all enjoy it with a clear conscience. It's blended malt, primarily from Clynelish, and bottled at 46%, has a natural colour and is non-chill filtered. By Compass Box's standards it's not particularly expensive and, as this is a sipping whisky that you'll linger over, a bottle may well last longer than you think.

Colour	Amber.
Nose	Quite floral and then spicy. Raisins, nuts and a suggestion of rosewater.
Taste	Brown bread, dark orange marmalade and brown sugar. Pronounced spice and wood notes; a bold and assertive whisky for sipping. Marzipan.
Finish	Complex and layered, this slips away slowly with the spice and full-bodied sweet vanilla hanging on for something of a crescendo!
Verdict	

94

Producer	Cooley Distillery PLC
Distillery	Cooley, Riverstown, Dundalk, Ireland
Visitor Centre	Yes – tours by appointment only
Availability	Specialists
Price	▢▪▢▢▢

www.tyrconnellwhiskey.com

The Tyrconnell

The resolutely independent Cooley Distillery was rewarded for its pioneering efforts with the award of World Distiller of the Year in 2008 and a staggering ten gold medals from the International Wine & Spirits Competition (IWSC) in 2009 (following nine the previous year).

All the more surprising then to learn that the distillery is, in fact, a converted potato alcohol plant bought in 1987 by the enterprising John Teeling and backed by some 300 shareholders. Two years of hard work followed, after which Cooley Distillery were able to fill their first cask in 1989.

However, The Tyrconnell has a much longer history and was once one of Ireland's best-known whiskeys. The company claim that, before Prohibition, it was among the best-selling Irish whiskey in the USA, pointing to advertising hoardings in the Yankee stadium in New York as evidence. The name, improbably enough, comes from the 100-1 winner of the Irish Classic horse race The National Produce Stakes which in 1876 was won by The Tyrconnell racehorse, owned by the Watts family of distillers. Delighted with this success a commemorative whiskey was launched, which charming story explains the splendid label with its delightful period feel, even if the 1762 date on the packaging is a little harder to justify.

The whiskey itself has been a mainstay for Cooley and today the range has been expanded to encompass extra-aged versions, various finishes and some single-cask offerings, the best of which are truly superb. But these are generally only in limited distribution and thus hard to find. What is more accessible is the standard non-aged Single Malt. I'm tempted to be a whisky know-all and suggest that this would be better bumped up to 46% abv and non-chill filtered, but this is a fine representative of the best of Irish distilling and a great advertisement for independent ownership.

Colour Pale – bourbon maturation at work here.
Nose Citrus and spice. Clean and appealing.
Taste Some honey, agreeably oily in the body, citrus tang appeals and spice. Medium body.
Finish Evolves agreeably with the principal characteristics showing well.

Verdict

95

Producer
Distillery
Visitor Centre
Availability
Price

Burn Stewart Distillers Ltd
Tobermory, Mull
Yes – tours by appointment
Specialists
▢▢▢▢▢

www.tobermorymalt.com

Tobermory
15 Years Old

There is something undeniably romantic about the idea of Tobermory distillery. For one thing, it's on an island. And, for another, it's small and has battled for survival against all the odds – the distillery was founded in 1798 (Barnard says 1823) but was 'silent' for long periods in the mid 1800s and 1930s, twice revived during the 1970s, then under threat of property development until it came into the ownership of Burn Stewart in 1993. So it would be nice if it could succeed.

But the kindest thing that one could say about much of the whisky, marketed alternately as Tobermory and Ledaig, is that the quality was variable. Frankly, to adapt the words of the poem, when it was good it was just about OK, but when it was bad it was horrid. I have had some shockers from this distillery. However, at last, there's some good news.

The whisky coming through now has been distilled by deeply committed long-term owners and under the guidance of the traditionally minded Ian McMillan, Burn Stewart's Master Blender and something of a zealot, the quality of Tobermory is much improved.

Nowhere is this seen more clearly than in this 15-year-old expression (it's no coincidence that the distillery changed hands 16 years ago), which is very much Ian's creation. The casks are stored mainly at Bunnahabhain where each year he selects a parcel of the best. These are re-racked in Gonzalez Byass sherry butts and sent back to Mull for a year's further maturation (there is very limited warehousing there) before it is bottled, non-chill filtered naturally, at 46.3% abv for loads of creamy mouth feel.

McMillan's marketing colleagues have also raised their game, with a nice bottle, handsome box and an interesting website. So, there you are – a good news story. Now try some!

Colour Rich deep gold.
Nose Plenty of sherry impact, dark orange marmalade and some suggestion of smoke.
Taste A medium body. Fruit cake, chocolate, vanilla toffees, light oak and some spice notes.
Finish Nuts, spice and salt.

Verdict

96

Producer	The Sazerac Company for J P Van Winkle & Son
Distillery	Buffalo Trace, Franklin County, Kentucky
Visitor Centre	Yes – but bear in mind this is the Buffalo Trace distillery and tours are designed with that in mind
Availability	You'll have to seek it out
Price	☐☐☐☐☐

www.oldripvanwinkle.com

Van Winkle

Family Reserve Rye

Rye? Why? You might be giving this entry some wry looks.
You might even think that Van Winkle is a daft name made up
by some marketing agency.

Wrong, wrong, wrong. Rye is whiskey's secret – the style that
refused to die. As the *International Herald Tribune* put it: 'Rye
whiskey is the world's great forgotten spirit, distinctive,
complex and delicious. It offers a tactile pleasure unlike any
other whiskey in the world.'

And the Van Winkle company can trace themselves back to the
late 1800s (which makes them American whiskey aristocracy)
when Julian P. 'Pappy' Van Winkle, Sr. was a travelling salesman
for the W.L. Weller and Sons wholesale house in Louisville,
hauling his samples round the state by horse and buggy.

After a complicated history (look it up if you're interested,
there's no space here) the company continues in the hands of
Julian Van Winkle III and his son, disappointingly named
Preston. Like so many other good things, their whiskies, mainly
soft, smooth, wheated bourbons, are made at the Buffalo Trace
Distillery near Louisville.

But this 13-year-old rye whiskey stands out. Rye isn't normally
aged that long and the result is a delightfully complex and
rewarding spirit that has seduced many experienced tasters.
Paul Pacult gave it 5 stars and scores don't go higher than that.
Grab a bottle and taste America's original whiskey.

Rye is probably what George Washington made. It's certainly
what the Whiskey Rebellion of 1794 was about – and, if
whiskey was worth fighting over, you can certainly go to the
trouble of tracking down a bottle.

Colour	Rich and warming, with copper hints and highlights.
Nose	Caramel and spice. Herbal nose of snuff.
Taste	Initially sweet, with toffee and leather. Rancio. Develops drying spice and pepper notes.
Finish	Dried fruits emphasise the complexity as this rich and powerful whiskey fades delightfully away.

Verdict

97

Producer | Austin, Nichols Distilling Co. (Campari Group)
Distillery | Wild Turkey, Lawrenceburg, Kentucky
Visitor Centre | Yes
Availability | Specialists
Price | ■■■□□

www.wildturkeybourbon.com

Wild Turkey

Rare Breed

There are a number of Wild Turkey variants – a standard version
at 8 years old; a number of aged versions; a rye; Russell's
Reserve, named after legendary Master Distiller Jimmy Russell;
and even a Honey Liqueur (with its own rather tacky 'American
Honey' calendar, from a creative team that apparently eats
regularly in Hooters and no doubt believes this the epitome of
upscale fine dining). All are good (with the possible exception of
the calendar) but I suggest you seek out some Wild Turkey Rare
Breed. It's a small batch Kentucky Straight Bourbon Whiskey,
blended from barrels at between 6 and 12 years of age and
bottled at barrel strength (54.1% abv).

The distillery has been through several hands: most recently it
was sold by Pernod Ricard to raise cash to pay for their Absolut
vodka purchase. It now belongs to the Italian Campari Group
(they also own Glen Grant in Scotland). At the time of writing
their plans for the brand are unclear but it would seem unlikely
that they will introduce fundamental change to a well-loved
bourbon icon, references to which appear regularly in popular
culture. Tours are available at the distillery.

This higher strength spirit can take the addition of some water
to open up the more delicate aromas, but go carefully. It does
not require significant dilution and may be best enjoyed as a
sipping whiskey, for those long evenings of contemplation –
unless, of course, raucous revelry is more to your taste. If you
do take a moment to contemplate, read the small booklet that
comes with the bottle and consider joining the Rare Breed
Society.

It's a marketing tool to help gather your contact information but,
for a brief moment, it's fun to pretend that you are a member of
a privileged elite 'who share Jimmy Russell's deep interest in
bourbon making and tasting'. Yee hah!

Colour Warm red to amber.
Nose High strength evident initially, then berries and
vanilla and toffee.
Taste Caramel, corn, liquorice, some citrus notes and
fresh red apples.
Finish Highly complex and layered, with a final kick.

Verdict

98

Producer	Brown-Forman Corporation
Distillery	Woodford Reserve, Versailles, Kentucky
Visitor Centre	Yes
Availability	Good in specialists and some supermarkets
Price	☐■☐☐☐

www.woodreserve.com

Woodford Reserve

Don't make the mistake of asking directions to Versailles in a European accent (as I once did). All you get from the locals are blank looks – it's 'Versales'! But when you get there some things at least will seem familiar – especially the still room.

And that's because the distinctive pot stills in which Woodford Reserve is distilled were manufactured in Rothes, Scotland, and shipped to Kentucky where a distiller from Scotland taught the locals how to use them.

Single batch bourbon was, in essence, the US's answer to the phenomenon of single malt Scotch and an attempt to make bourbon, which had acquired a blue-collar image, chic once again. Well, it's worked and Woodford Reserve was one of the first to show that it could be done.

The parent company, Brown-Forman Corporation (who also own Jack Daniel's), invested around $14m in restoring the old Labrot & Graham distillery which they had owned for 30 years from 1941. They sold it in 1971, bought it back in 1994, turned it into a showpiece, and rebranded it as Woodford Reserve.

At first the product closely resembled another B-F brand, Old Forester, but today it's a vatting of some column still whiskey with the output of the L&G pot stills, made in small batches.

The distillery, which is on an unusual boutique scale for the USA, has a fine visitor centre. Great stress is laid on the limestone spring water, cypress fermentation vessels, small pot stills and stone warehouses. The result is a Kentucky classic, with many fans.

Colour	Dark honey.
Nose	Vanilla sweetness, honey, fresh fruits and hints of chocolate.
Taste	Rich and warming, with layers of mint, tobacco, leather and fruit. Smooth and full bodied. Will seem sweet to the European palate.
Finish	Smooth and warming; very consistent and balanced.

Verdict

99

Producer	Suntory
Distillery	Yamazaki, near Osaka, Honshu Island, Japan
Visitor Centre	Yes – rated as one of the best in the world and it also has an excellent whisky museum
Availability	Good in specialists, some supermarkets carry younger ages
Price	☐■☐☐☐

www.theyamazaki.jp

Yamazaki

12 Years Old

Look out Scotland! Wake up!

There used to be an arrogance in Scotland about Japanese whisky, best summed up in a Scotch Whisky Association publication of 1951: 'The Japs came to this country years ago, copied our plant and even employed some of our Speyside personnel. They produced an imitation of Speyside Whisky which was not good although drinkable.'

Such patronising attitudes die hard and may be observed to this day. To those who hold them I say, 'Look at the British car industry – then be afraid, be very afraid.'

The fact is that the best Japanese whisky is very, very good and very, very Japanese. Yes, their restlessly innovative, quality-obsessed producers copied the best of Scottish practice, but then they adapted and improved it for Japanese conditions. As a result, Japanese whisky is collecting prizes, winning medals and growing fast. In the four years to 2007, Yamazaki's European sales grew 23 times. From a small base, admittedly, but it can't be ignored. In fact, whiskies like this should be celebrated.

The original Japanese malt distillery, Yamazaki was founded in 1923 at the site of a famous water source where three rivers converge. The distillery is often shrouded in mist and the warehouses sit sheltered by a bamboo forest. Japanese distillers don't swap 'fillings' for their blends with rivals so the stills at Yamazaki are all different in size and shape, permitting a bewildering range of styles to be produced.

Try any you can find. There are other Japanese whiskies listed here but this one is a favourite and a great, good-value introduction to a whole other world of whisky.

Colour Gold.
Nose Vanilla, cloves and panettone.
Taste Medium bodied. Sweet, then spicy. Honey and lemon. Dried fruits. Wood.
Finish Dry and spicy.

Verdict

100

Producer	Suntory
Distillery	Yamazaki, near Osaka, Honshu Island, Japan
Visitor Centre	Yes – rated as one of the best in the world and it also has an excellent whisky museum
Availability	Good in specialists and some supermarkets carry younger ages
Price	▢■■▢▢

www.theyamazaki.jp

Yamazaki
18 Years Old

In 1923, Shinjiro Torii, the founder of Suntory and a pioneer of Japanese whisky, built Japan's first malt whisky distillery in the Vale of Yamazaki. Using copper pot stills, the Yamazaki distillery was the first of its kind outside of Scotland. The distillery's location on the outskirts of Japan's ancient capital of Kyoto offered pure waters, diversity of climate and high humidity – the ideal environment for the maturation of good whisky.

Today, Suntory's Yamazaki is the most popular single malt whisky in Japan and is enjoyed by whisky connoisseurs in more than 25 countries. The visitor centre at Yamazaki is also very popular attracting around 100,000 visitors annually for the free, 90-minute guided tour.

This older version of Yamazaki is relatively easy to find in the UK. However, if you find that you like it, there are also a number of limited releases and special finishes – though, these are generally more expensive and/or harder to find. The extra age has changed this whisky quite markedly, adding depth and distinction to the flavour. Where the 12-year-old is pleasantly light, this has extra body and additional complexity, without in any way feeling over-aged. By any standard, it's an impressive and enjoyable whisky.

In the UK Suntory own Morrison Bowmore and therefore have achieved quite widespread distribution in larger supermarkets, specialists and whisky bars. They have been active in entering competitive tastings and this 18 Years Old expression has won major awards from the International Wine & Spirits Competition, San Francisco World Spirits Competition and the Beverage Tasting Institute.

Colour Copper gold.

Nose Black cherry seems to be a Yamazaki signature, also some oakiness, sherry, and the age is evident.

Taste Fuller than the 12 Years. Toffee. Earthy, dusty, rooty – it's wood, Jock, but not as we know it. Dried fruits, moss and bark (but no bite).

Finish Quite satisfyingly long and consistent. Some commentators get pomegranate. I don't.

Verdict

101

Producer	Nikka
Distillery	Yoichi, Hokkaido, Japan
Visitor Centre	Yes
Availability	Specialists
Price	☐☐■☐☐

www.nikka.com

Yoichi

10 Years Old

This is one of the really great whisky stories – a fitting end to this exploration of 101 whiskies to try before you die.

The company that today we know as Nikka was founded in July 1934 when Masataka Taketsuru bought a large parcel of reclaimed land by the Yoichi River, a site he recognised as being ideal for producing whisky in a Scottish style. This had been his dream since studying distilling in Scotland from 1918–20 (during which time he also married Scots girl Rita Cowan). He returned to Japan in 1920 and helped establish the Yamazaki distillery.

But he wanted to build, own and operate his own 'Scottish' distillery in Japan and, as such, he is widely honoured as the 'father' of Japanese whisky. Today Yoichi is owned by Asahi Breweries but continues to operate in a highly traditional manner, with direct-firing of the spirit stills and worm tubs for condensing the spirit. As elsewhere in Japan, the distillery can adapt quickly to differing styles of whisky, as a result of which no spirit from outside the company is required for blending.

Taketsuru managed the company through World War 2, its merger with Asahi and the development of the company's Sendai distillery in 1969. He eventually died in 1979, aged 85. In 1989 Nikka acquired the Ben Nevis distillery in Fort William, Scotland, and restarted production there, thus completing a kind of a circle in this remarkable man's contribution to the history and development of whisky in both Japan and Scotland.

There are several expressions available but the most accessible in the UK is this 10-year-old style. Various 'Nikka' branded malts are also seen, some of which contain whisky from Yoichi (e.g. Nikka Black and Nikka Taketsuru pure malts). Drink any of these and raise your glass to a true visionary and pioneer, who really tried before he died.

Colour Deep bronze.
Nose Bold and direct, with peat evident. Light citrus notes.
Taste Minty chocolate and orange oil. Creamy mouth feel and delicate peat smoke.
Finish Sweetness, peat and some antiseptic notes in alternate waves.

Verdict

How to taste whisky and use this book

Tasting whisky – any whisky – is straightforward. Follow these simple rules to get the most from your dram.

1. Use the right glass. A tumbler is hopeless. What you need is the Glencairn Crystal whisky glass (buy online from www.glencairn.co.uk). If you can't find those, get a sherry copita or brandy snifter to concentrate volatile aromas and help you 'nose' the whisky.

2. Fix the aroma and taste with associations – the smell of new-mown grass, for example, a vanilla-flavoured toffee or the rich taste of fruit cake.

3. Add a little water. It opens up the spirit and prevents your taste buds from becoming numbed by alcohol.

4. Roll the whisky right round your mouth and 'chew' it. Give the flavours time to develop: the whisky has been ageing for years – give it as least as many seconds and the rewards will be huge.

5. Finally, think about the 'finish', or the lingering taste that remains. How consistent is it? What new flavours emerge?

Relax, keep practising and you'll very soon discover whisky's unique richness.

Imagine you were about to make a trip to a foreign land. Use this book as a sort of traveller's guide to the new country: it points you to some sights that you didn't know were there or might otherwise have ignored on your journey. I don't claim to have all the answers; I don't know what whisky you like and there's no reason at all to assume that you'll like the same whiskies as me. That's why there are no scores here. But you can be assured that every whisky here is here for a reason and that they are good, often great, whiskies of their kind.

So try them at least once. Before you die.

Acknowledgements

My wife, Lindsay, has been enormously patient and put up with my grumpy moods and mental absences while writing this book. Presumably she's used to it by now. Worryingly, she claims that she didn't notice any difference. Either way, the biggest thanks go to her.

My agent, Judy Moir, believed in the book from the start and was positive, helpful and encouraging. Her husband, Neville, helped as well: he knows what he did! Thanks to both of them and to Bob McDevitt at Hachette for his enthusiasm and support. Jo Roberts-Miller did a great job editing the book in double-quick time.

I ruthlessly exploited most of my contacts in the wonderful world of whisky by asking them to nominate their three 'Desert Island Drams', without revealing the purpose of the enquiry. This group includes distillers, blenders, whisky writers, retailers, company directors and visitor centre guides – anyone, in fact, who seems to me to talk sense about whisky and was able and willing to offer some insights. The real reason, of course, was to ensure that I didn't miss anything out. Their cumulative wisdom drew my attention to many gems.

In alphabetical order my 'oracles' were:

Russell Anderson, Raymond Armstrong, Helen Arthur, Dave Broom, Jonathan Brown, Chris Bunting, Frank Coleman, Yves Cosentino, Ronnie Cox, Jason Craig, Katherine Crisp, Jim Cryle, Kathleen Di Benedetto, Dr Clemens Dillmann, Duncan Elphick, Kevin Erskine, James Espey, Graham Eunson, Michael Fraser-Milne, John Glaser, Peter Gordon, Lawrence Graham, Alan Gray, Ken Grier, Teimei Horiuchi, Professor Paul Hughes, David Hume, Barrie Jackson, Richard Joynson, Naofumi Kamiguchi, Mike Keiller, Iain Kennedy, David King, John Lamond, Bill Lark, Jim Long, Mhairi MacDonald, Neil MacDonald, Ian MacIlwain, Charlie MacLean, Ian MacMillan, Nial Mackinlay, Anabel Meikle, Marcin Miller, Tatsuya Minagawa, Philip Morrice, Peter Muller, Peter Mulryan, David Nathan-Maister, Stuart Nickerson, Alex Nicol, Martine Nouet, Becky Offringa, Hans Offringa, Bill Owens, Richard Paterson, Brett Pontoni, Vijay Rekhi, Ken Robertson, Ingvar Ronde, Dominic Roskrow, Franz Scheurer, Colin Scott, Jacqui Seargeant, Sukhinder Singh, Gavin D Smith, Stuart Smith, David Stewart, Steven Sturgeon, Jack Teeling, Luke Tegner, Jeffrey Topping, Misako Udo, Kerry Walsh Skerry, Iain Weir, Neil Wilson, Alan Winchester, David Wishart, Ian Wisniewski and Graham Wright.

My thanks to all of them.

Further resources

Books

There are many, many books and websites about whisky; some would say too many. However, I have suggested just a few here for further reading, the idea being (like the list of whiskies) to point you in various directions in the pursuit of knowledge.

The first modern book written about whisky was Aeneas MacDonald's *Whisky*, reissued in facsimile in 2006. Despite its age (it first appeared in 1930) it is well worth reading as a poetic general introduction to Scotch whisky that is still surprisingly relevant.

For the history of the Scotch whisky industry Michael Moss and John Hume's *The Making of Scotch Whisky* is valuable, though dry and now somewhat dated. *Scotch Whisky – A Liquid History* by Charles Maclean is rather easier going. Any title by Charlie is worth reading.

Gavin D. Smith is very strong on the people and personalities in Scotch. Look out for *The Whisky Men*. For taste evaluation of Scotch whiskies try *Whisky Classified* by David Wishart.

There is very little in English on Japanese whisky. Perhaps the most authoritative is *Japanese Whisky: Facts, Figures and Taste* by Ulf Buxrud. It does what it says in the title. If there is a really good book on American whiskies it has passed me by and an up-to-date account of Irish whiskey is badly needed.

For more comprehensive coverage of all world whiskies and a basic introduction, look for *World Whisky* edited by Charles MacLean. I was one of a number of contributors. The new edition of the late Michael Jackson's *Malt Whisky Companion* has been compiled by Dominic Roskrow and Gavin D. Smith and is exhaustive. Some people find Jim Murray's annual *Whisky Bible* useful. He tastes almost everything!

The *Malt Whisky Yearbook* is issued annually and covers more than just single malt. It is an invaluable guide; accurate, regularly updated and a mine of interesting information, especially on new distilleries.

A tiny little company called Classic Expressions, which I run with a colleague, reprints rare collectable classics of whisky writing in numbered limited editions – www.classicexpressions.co.uk.

There are various magazines. Perhaps the best (in English) are *Whisky Magazine* (UK) and its American counterpart *The Malt Advocate*.

Websites
There are literally hundreds, perhaps thousands, of websites on whisky, ranging from the exhaustive to the scanty, the authoritative and reliable to the frankly eccentric. Bloggers come and go and maintain their sites with different levels of enthusiasm and accuracy. Virtually every brand of note maintains its own site: if you read between the PR lines there may be some useful information.

Given that the web evolves and changes both rapidly and constantly, the following recommendations may be of limited value. However, for what it is worth, I do look at these sites fairly regularly. Apologies to those that I have missed or forgotten about. A few hours 'googling' will turn up more whisky sites than you thought possible. Good luck!

www.irelandwhiskeytrail.com (exactly what you'd expect with that name)

www.maltmadness.com (set aside a good chunk of time if you venture here)

www.maltmaniacs.org (I can't imagine how they find the time to keep this up!)

www.nonjatta.blogspot.com (reports in English from Japan)

www.ralfy.com (this is great fun)

www.whiskycast.com (authoritative whisky podcasts)

www.whiskyfun.com ('it's about single malts, music, enjoying life in general')

www.whiskyintelligence.com (news updates and press releases)

www.whisky-pages.com (Gavin D. Smith's tasting notes and reviews)

Where to buy

There are now a great number of off-licences (liquor stores) all round the world that trade as whisky specialists, and many of them are excellent, with knowledgeable and enthusiastic staff. I can think of examples as far away as Switzerland, Singapore, New Zealand and, of course, the USA. New ones are springing up all the time as whisky grows in popularity and the choice they offer can be deliciously bewildering. In the interests of my sanity though, this section is restricted to the UK, where fortunately for us we are spoilt for choice with excellent specialist whisky retailers. The following have particularly good online shopping facilities:

Royal Mile Whiskies, Edinburgh
www.royalmilewhiskies.com

The Whisky Exchange, London
www.thewhiskyexchange.com

Loch Fyne Whiskies, Inveraray
www.lochfynewhiskies.co.uk

But ideally you should browse and talk to some enthusiastic and well-informed staff. There are many more good shops, notably The Whisky Shop (UK wide), The Wee Dram (Bakewell, Derbyshire), Lincoln Whisky Shop, The Whisky Shop (Dufftown), The Whisky Castle (Tomintoul), Arkwrights (Highworth, Wiltshire), Parkers of Banff, Robert Grahams (Glasgow), Whiskies of Scotland (Huntly), Nickolls & Perks (Stourbridge) and Luvians (St Andrews).

Above all, Gordon & MacPhail's shop in Elgin is a shrine and well worth a visit. See their entry in the 101.

In London you will find The Whisky Exchange, Royal Mile Whiskies, Berry Bros & Rudd, Milroy's of Soho and The Vintage House. Nationally, the better Oddbins stores have a good selection of whisky and they have a good website, too.

Picture credits

The author and publisher would like to thank the following for supplying the photographs in the book. Every effort has been made to fulfil requirements with regard to reproducing copyright material. The author and publisher will be glad to rectify any omissions at the earliest opportunity.

Incidental imagery

Page 6	The Spencerfield Spirits Company	Page 216	The BenRiach Distillery
Page 12	Highland Park	Page 218	Highland Park

Whisky imagery

Aberfeldy 21	Bacardi Global Brand Ltd	Hedonism	Compass Box Whisky
Aberlour a'bunadh	Chivas Brothers	Hibiki 17	Suntory Liquor Ltd
Amrut Fusion	Amrut Distilleries Ltd	Hibiki 30	Suntory Liquor Ltd
anCnoc 16	Burt Greener Communications	Highland Park 18	Highland Park
Ardbeg 10	The Glenmorangie Company	Highland Park 21	Highland Park
Ardbeg Uigeadail	The Glenmorangie Company	Highland Park 30	Highland Park
Asyla	Compass Box Whisky	Highland Park 40	Highland Park
Auchentoshan Classic	Morrison Bowmore Distillers	Isle of Jura Superstition	White & MacKay
Balblair '89	Burt Greener Communications	Jameson -	
Ballantines 17	Chivas Brothers	Limited Reserve 18	Irsih Distillers Pernod Ricard
Basil Hayden's	Beam Global Spirits & Wine	Johnnie Walker Black	Diageo plc
BenRiach	The BenRiach Distillery	Johnnie Walker Blue KGV	Diageo plc
Benromach Organic	Benromach Speyside Single Malt Scotch Whisky	Kilchoman	Kichoman Distillery
		Knob Creek	Beam Global Spirits & Wine
Bernheim Original Wheat	Heaven Hill Distilleries, Inc.	Lagavulin 16	Diageo plc
Black Bottle	Alan Stewart Photography	Laphroaig Quarter Cask	Lime PR
Black Grouse	The Black Grouse	Longrow CV	Springbank Distilleries Ltd
Bladnoch 8	Bladnoch Distillery	Mackmyra	Johan Olsson
Blue Hanger	Berry Bros. & Rudd Spirits	Maker's Mark	The Whisky Exchange
BNJ Bailie Nicol Jarvie	The Glenmorangie Company	Mellow Corn	Heaven Hill Distilleries, Inc.
Bowmore Tempest	Morrison Bowmore Distillers	Monkey Shoulder	William Grant & Sons Distillers
Bruichladdich 12	Bruichladdich Distillery	Mortlach 16	Diageo plc
Buffalo Trace	Buffalo Trace Distillery	Nikka All Malt	Asahi Breweries, Ltd
Bunnahabhain 18	C&H Creative	Oban 14	Diageo plc
Bushmills 16	Diageo plc	Old Pulteney 17	Burt Greener Communications
Cameron Brig	The Whisky Exchange	Redbreast 12	Irsih Distillers Pernod Ricard
Caol Ila 12	Diageo plc	Scapa	Chivas Brothers
Chivas Regal 25	Chivas Brothers	Smokehead Extra Black	Ian MacLeod Distillers
Clynelish 14	Diageo plc	Speyburn Solera 25	Burt Greener Communications
Crown Royal	Diageo plc	Springbank 10	Springbank Distilleries Ltd
Cutty Sark	Berry Bros. & Rudd Spirits	Talisker 10	Diageo plc
Cutty Sark 25	Berry Bros. & Rudd Spirits	Talisker 18	Diageo plc
Dalmore 12	White & MacKay	The Balvenie 21	William Grant & Sons Distillers
Dalwhinnie 15	Diageo plc	The Balvenie 30	William Grant & Sons Distillers
Deanston 12	Salkeld Photography	The Glenrothes -	
Dewar's 12	Bacardi Global Brand Ltd	Select Reserve	The Glenrothes
Dewar's Signature	Bacardi Global Brand Ltd	The Macallan 10	The Macallan Distillery Ltd
Eagle Rare	Buffalo Trace Distillery	The Macallan 18	The Macallan Distillery Ltd
Elijah Craig 12	Heaven Hill Distilleries, Inc.	The Macallan 30	The Macallan Distillery Ltd
Glen Breton	Glenora Distilleries	The Society's Special -	
Glenfarclas 105	J&G Grant	Highland Blend	Brendan MacNeill
Glenfarclas 21	J&G Grant	The Spice Tree	Compass Box Whisky
Glenfiddich 18	William Grant & Sons Distillers	Thomas H Handy -	
Glenfiddich 30	William Grant & Sons Distillers	Sazerac Straight Rye	Buffalo Trace Distillery
Glenglassaugh 26	Anne Smith	Tobermory 15	Good Creative
Glenglassaugh Spirit Drink	Anne Smith	Tyrconnell	Cooley Distillery
Glengoyne 21	Ian MacLeod Distillers	Van Winkle Family -	
Glenlivet 21	Chivas Brothers	Reserve Rye	Buffalo Trace Distillery
Glenmorangie -		Wild Turkey	The Whisky Exchange
Quinta Ruban	The Glenmorangie Company	Woodford Reserve	Woodford Reserve Distillery
Gordon & MacPhail -		Yamazaki 12	Suntory Liquor Ltd
Glen Grant 25	Gordon & MacPhail	Yamazaki 18	Suntory Liquor Ltd
Green Spot	Mitchell & Son	Yoichi 10	Asahi Breweries, Ltd
Hakushu 18	Suntory Liquor Ltd